"Jambia"

is
A Novel by
by
David John Hay

All characters in this novel are fictitious.
They maybe amalgams of people I have
known, altered for dramatic effect; or
people that I have conjured from my
imagination.

For Sally & John
Enjoy my imagination
David 5-5-19

Acknowledgements

I wish to acknowledge the assistance of Judi Rastall of Sutton-on-Sea, Lincolnshire. I could not have finished this edition without her critical eye.

I would also like to thank Hendrik Grzebatzki of Duisburg, Germany for taking the portrait of the author to be found on the rear cover.

The front cover design is by the author, David Hay (19/08/18)

1.

"How do you stop the British killing Moslems?"
Tariq lay on his bed reading. A total stranger was framed in the doorway.
"They," Tariq lifted his chin to indicate the smoke detector, "Can hear what you say."
"Don't worry." The visitor waved a small remote. "This jams listening devices. It's safe to talk."
"Are you sure?"
"The camera is pointing in your room. I'm in the doorway. They can't see me. But you must look busy."
Tariq looked down at the Quran, open across his lap,
"You know," Began the stranger, "Christian terrorist attacked for many years. The IRA bombed London and Birmingham…"
"Brighton…" added Tariq.
"Yes," The newcomer smiled, "Attacking the British government. But it didn't scare them."
"Stiff upper lip." Tariq enjoyed the idiom.
"Exactly," he agreed. "London Underground attack didn't strike terror in their hearts."
"Business as usual…" Tariq was warming to the topic.
"Precisely. So, what would stop them?"
"Islamic State killing all infidels."
"The attacks on their cities do not stop them. So what would stop the UK from killing Moslems… forever."
The younger man touched his Quran. "They must follow the words of Allah."
"Al-hum-dull-Allah! In the end. But what is the first step to making this a caliphate?"
"You tell me."
"Chernobyl?"

"What is that?"

"A Ukrainian city. A nuclear power station blew up."

"A bomb?"

"No. An accident."

"An accident?"

"And still no one can live there."

"What are you saying?"

"Soon you will make the ultimate sacrifice. You will cause many, many such accidents. Then this country cannot kill any more Moslem children. They won't kill any more Moslem women. We'll stop them killing our Moslem brothers."

"Al-hum-dull-Allah," Tariq reacted. "Allah be praised. When?"

"Soon." The older man glanced at his watch. "I will contact you through your brother at the Brixton Mosque at Zuhr Prayer on Friday."

The black-suited foreigner stepped across the hallway into the tiny upstairs bathroom. He bolted the door then switched off the jamming device. He wanted the listeners to think it had only been a small technical glitch.

Tariq glanced at the doorway. He heard the bolt. Next the visitor pulled the chain. After which, he stomped downstairs.

It had been over eight months since Tariq had talked to anyone outside his immediate family. He recalled that thin aesthetic face, receding hairline and the Saddam Hussein moustache. His imagination was fired up imagining the accidents, the attacks to make the accidents happen. No need to import expensive weapons. They were going to make accidents happen. Islamic State was clever like that.

Then he began to wonder how he could take part, when he was tagged. But if he was instrumental in preventing Britain from attacking Moslem countries, then he was prepared to make the ultimate sacrifice.

"Al-hum-dull-Allah."

2.

Faisal Khan cycled to work whenever he could. He arrived with time to shower and change into one of the two identical grey suits from his locker. Once transformed into a stereotypical civil servant, he took the elevator to the third floor. Turning left, he stepped briskly to the last door on the right. He knocked once and entered.

Reception was manned by the only openly transvestite identical twins in MI5. This morning they were in their male personas.
"Good morning Michael... Francis. Splendid day." Faisal leant forward and gazed into the eye scanner, waiting for the security door to open.
"Good morning Mr Khan," chirped Michael. "Yes it is."
The door slid open and Faisal stepped into the vestibule. This was the only access to their section of the building. There were several such self-contained units at Thames House. Theirs was nicknamed 'The Syrian Desk'. He turned as the semi-circular door swished round him, opening up the large open-plan office, at the same time closing off the outside world.

Several of his colleagues were already at their stations. He went to his desk and switched on the computer and monitor. Then he wandered across to the coffee machine, chatting to fellow Intelligence Officers on route. He waved to his Project Manager, Josephine Pullen, in her space, a recess beside the store room. Coffee in hand, Faisal returned to his station, put in his earpiece and attached the microphone to his lapel. Then he went through his morning routine; checking the recordings from the tagged 'Syrians', both aural and visual.

Half an hour later he gestured to the Section Head as she moved through the office.
"Lord Leyton visited Tariq Siddiqi's place yesterday afternoon."
Jo moved nearer and stood gazing at his screen.
"What's he doing with one of our Syrian Asbos?"
"According to his tag," Faisal informed her, "Tariq remained in his bedroom throughout the visit."
"Why did his lordship go there?"
"As far as I can tell, he stayed in the kitchen with Tariq's mum."
"How do you know?"
"They barely stop talking."
"What did they talk about?"
"She's trying to persuade the courts her son isn't a terrorist."
"Yea. Right-on babe."
"There is an irregularity though."
"An irregularity?"
He switched the computer speakers on. "Listen."

They could hear the distorted, echoing conversation in the kitchen, then a babble of sound. "It lasts for 3.19 minutes."

"What caused that?" Jo wondered.

"I can't separate it. This could be a new sophisticated device."

"Or a blip," she suggested.

"Or a blip," he agreed.

"What do they want to hide?"

"Mrs Siddiqi?" Faisal questioned. "She's religious, but not political. Not very intellectually stimulating for his lordship, I would think."

"Don't be sexist."

"No. I didn't mean that. It is just she is narrow in her...."

"OK. I believe you. See if Tom can separate the sound for you. OK?"

"Yeh. It maybe nothing, but... you never know."

3.

Jasmine Siddiqi was still wearing her school uniform as she left Brixton tube station. She was on her lunch break and wanted to complete the round trip back to school, in time. The willowy teenager turned left and walked briskly past Iceland, along the arcade of small shops until she came to the dark passage between the shops.

She paused to look at herself in a shop window, ostensibly to adjust her headscarf and long black skirt, but at the same time glancing back along her route. Nobody appeared to be following her. She moved through the arched passageway; then turned right, along the alleyway behind the shops. Coming to a peeling pale green gate, Jazz peeked over her shoulder before clicking the stiff metal latch.

She was in a back yard cluttered with the debris of a small business: wooden pallets, some cardboard tied in bundles, plastic shapes and looping coils of wire from packing crates and three huge refuse bins. Flies buzzed round these smelly containers. The schoolgirl held her scarf across her nose as she stepped wearily between the rubbish piles. She made her way to the back door. It was the same shade of peeling sun-bleached green. The door knob turned easily. She casually looked round before disappearing inside.

Darren Robbins sat at a desk in his bedroom above the family café. Being in the Upper Sixth he was entitled to leave of absence when not in lessons. He was fully engrossed in his studies, determined to get as much done as possible before Jazz popped in for lunch.

He was not going to end up like his parents, scrimping and saving all his life for the essential. He was determined to get a university place, despite the cost. He wanted a proper job in the IT, hopefully in the gaming industry. There was a lot of money to be made and he wanted part of it. At least that had been the plan before he met Jasmine. Although she was only a fifth year, he found her really mature for her years. At least that is what he told his parents. They knew Darren was besotted. He was head over heels in love with her.

"Dazz?" She whispered from the doorway. It was as though his finger touched the light socket. He shot out of the chair sending it crashing to the floor.

"Jazz." His voice was squeaky.

She laughed and strode confidently into the room,

"What cha' doing?"

"I'm..." He was embarrassed by his crassness, "You know. Got any?"

"Yeh. Will you help me with it, pretty please?"

She deftly unwound the scarf and let her lustrous black hair cascade across her shoulders. She moved her head from side to side and it shimmered. She could feel his adoring eyes on her.

"What is it?" He asked.

"What is what?" She moved very close to him.

"Your..." Again his voice squeaked, "Your homework."

"I will tell you... but first I want a kiss."

Their lips locked together. His hands clumsily travelled up and down her back. They ventured tentatively onto her firm buttocks. After a short while her hands stopped caressing his neck to firmly re-attach his hands on her waistline and she grinned against his teeth as the kiss continued.

4.

By pushing a button on the armrest, Lord Kabir Anwar of Leyton opened the glass partition to the chauffeur. They were driving in his favourite burgundy Bentley Silver Spur V8. They were travelling west towards the Palace of Westminster. He cleared his throat. Suleiman Al Dossari turned an ear tactfully towards his employer.

"That was enlightening," Lord Kabir reminisced.

"Yes Your Lordship."

"Visiting these families. Can you believe that her son has been under house arrest for eight months? And no trial in sight," he sighed wistfully, "We really must try to help

9

these people. They are being turned into pariahs by the British media."

"Yes Your Lordship."

"As you know, I'm attending the Commission for Nuclear Power meeting at The Department of Energy & Climate Change at two. We should be finished at four."

"Yes Your Lordship."

"Then take me home. Tomorrow I will go to Gayhurst Manor. I want to see how much progress is being made. It's cost me an arm and a leg. I want to see how it's being spent."

"Of course, Your Lordship." The partition began to slide shut, but stopped.

"Oh yes. I'm going to Brighton on Friday. Taking some of my peers on a trip to France for lunch. Ha! Some of my peers…"

He chuckled as the partition slid shut. In the silence Suleiman tapped number eight on the satnav keypad. That would take them safely to his lordship's meeting, avoiding any recent holdups.

The chauffeur knew he had to work quickly while the aristocrat was engaged in his conference. He had to warn 'the trainers' of the 'surprise' visit the following day. He would also need to make a few calls to take full advantage of the cross Channel trip the day after that.

Unfortunately he was not privy to his lordship's diary, so had little warning of the peer's movements. They had waited over three weeks for this opportunity and it could well be another three or four weeks before they would have another chance to bring their ballistic expert in. It was now or never.

As he drove through the lunchtime traffic, his mind was rehearsing the pending telephone conversations. He had to be succinct. There may be listeners. He was aware of the tight timetable they were all working towards. Not much time to synchronise these sudden leaps forward. Nevertheless, it was essential to keep everything on schedule.

5.

Faisal finished scanning the recordings from his Syrians and went back to the coffee machine. He had listened to Tariq's recording several times but his software could not get beyond that noise. It was not the usual 'white noise' that these devices emitted. This was more like a cacophony of sound. An actual noise. Really challenging. Much to his frustration, he could not crack this on his own. He needed a more sophisticated programme than his computer was authorised to run.

Thomas Canning was the Syrian Desk's residential Digital Intelligence Tactical Solutions Developer allocated for his IT skills rather than his experience as a field officer. He was established in the opposite corner of the office, from the Section Head's space. It was the furthest point from her. Also, although he faced the room, Tom was hidden behind a bank of monitors and electronic hardware. He was overweight and blinked owlishly through thick lenses as Tom cleared his throat,
"You busy Tom?"
"Ominous! What do you want? Is it urgent?"
"Whatever we do, it's always urgent. You ought to know that."

"Tell me about it. Everyone expects me to drop what I'm doing and take on whatever they think is urgent. Pisses me off at times."

"You're just not loved enough…"

"Alright. No need to be sarkie."

"I just thought you might find this intriguing…"

"What?" Despite himself, the technician was becoming interested,

"Just sounds like a new sort of jamming device, that's all."

"What does?"

"You will have to come to my station."

Reluctantly Thomas heaved himself off the complaining computer chair. He waddled after the more nimble Intelligence Officer. Once there he put the earpiece in and listened intently. Faisal played the interrupted section. And Faisal was right. Tom was intrigued.

Agent Canning toddled back to his station to collect a memory stick. Faisal noticed that he was breathing heavily when he returned. While he was copying the relevant piece, his tongue ran backwards and forwards along his lower lip.

"I don't think it is just a blip at all."

"Why not?"

"Doesn't sound right. More like a transmitted sound."

"What can we do?"

Tom withdrew the stick from Faisal's machine and padded back to his area.

"Not sure yet. I'll scan it with my software first."

"How long will it take?"

Tom stopped so abruptly that Faisal bumped into him. They both looked surprised.

"How long is a piece of string?"

"Just wanted to know if I should stand next to you. Or get another coffee. Or maybe get on with something else. That's all."

"Get on with something else."

And with that Tom continued to his station and Faisal returned to his.

6.

They pulled off the M1 at Junction 14. It was signposted to Milton Keynes. Suleiman slowed for the roundabout below the motorway and onto the A509 towards Newport Pagnell. The drive from London had been uneventful. They made good time on the motorway despite the long sections controlled by average speed cameras.

Within fifteen minutes they pulled into the short drive across the dry moat. They were in front of imposing heavy-duty wooden doors, filling the arched brickwork gatehouse of Gayhurst Manor. Suleiman lowered his window. He leaned towards the speaker unit set in the brickwork to the right of the gates.

"Lord Kabir Anwar of Leyton," Suleiman announced to the intercom. The gates juddered then slowly swung inwards, one at a time.

As soon as the space was wide enough, the Bentley Silver Spur purred into the inner courtyard. It negotiated the circular drive with a fountain in the middle. Subtle coloured lights played in the spout of water as it gurgled happily in the peace of the piazza. The gates closed behind them, shutting out any preying eyes.

In front of them stood the imposing three-storey, modern brick built manor house. While on the other three sides were 'stables'. Above the two-story high gate house sat a small clock tower with a clock face looking inward. It comprised of two rooms above a large archway with the door set on the outside. A vehicle could park inside the quad, under the arch, out of the weather. Suleiman walked round the car to open the rear door. His lordship ducked out of the limousine and stood looking up at the manor house for a while before declaring, "Splendid."

After closing the gates, Naveed Nazir strode towards his visitors. He was wearing a long grey and white striped Djellaba and Kufi Topi, the laced skull cap of a Moslem. He was clean shaven which was unusual for one so devout. "So sorry we are not ready to receive you," he blurted to his benefactor.

"No problem," he used conciliatory tones. "I was just passing, so I thought I'd pop in and see what progress you have made."

Naveed beckoned them to follow. He went towards the stables on the left which had been transformed into a mechanical workshop. There were two concrete pits and four fully equipped benches. Shiny new tools glinted under the fluorescent lights. To the extreme right a white Ford Transit 280 SWB 2.2TDCi stood waiting attention. Its roof had been cut off and was propped against the far wall.

"We are beginning soon," Naveed explained. "We want our students to see the inside of the vehicle... before they can fix it."

His lordship nodded sagely, mesmerised by a ring-spanner set hanging on hooks against their individual shapes on the tool board attached to the wall. One spanner was missing. Its outline shape seemed strangely empty. Like an accusation.

"Now," The guide suggested, "Let's look at the student accommodation."

He led the way into the sunlight. They crossed the courtyard to climb the steps into the main building. Lord Kabir insisted on looking into every room inside the manor. There were twelve bedrooms, each equipped with twin beds, a set of drawers and double wardrobes.

Then he met Ibrahim Caan and Hussain Ahmed in the kitchen. They were wiping down an already spotless worktop having prepared lunch.

"You must stay for Zuhr Prayer. Then share our midday meal."

"I cannot. You do not have enough food."

"Believe me," Naveed interrupted, "Ibrahim can create a feast in the desert."

Ibrahim smiled and bowed repeatedly to their patron.

"OK," his Lordship relented. "Let me see. What will the students eat?"

"They eat what we eat." Ibrahim declared, "Like this…"

He gestured to the table, "I have prepared Aloo Matar Ki Sabzi, Chatori Daal, some charcoal grilled chicken and Chawal."

"It sounds absolutely delicious. Do the students eat this well?"

"Of course," Naveed replied smoothly. "A student with a full stomach is a happy learner."

The small group of men made their way into the spacious dining room. They were offered Qehwa and Lassi to drink, while they patiently waited for the prayer time.

7.

15

The Controller held his weekly briefing every Thursday at 10:00. His predecessor had always met on Friday afternoon, which was often the busiest day of the week and everyone was tired by then. Meetings became routine rather than useful, rubber stamping the management and woe betide anyone who asked a question. Like any changes, some people liked them while most did not.

Jo Pullen was a new member of the management team had no strong opinions. This was all she had ever known. She had no firm opinions either way. It was unusual to make her level appointment from outside Thames House. But she had moved from an administration role in the Foreign Office to become Project Manager for Monitoring Terrorists for Thames House.

She went down ten minutes early to pick up some freshly ground coffee from the canteen en route. When she arrived, most other section heads were taking their seats round the oval-shaped highly polished oak boardroom table.

"I think we are all here," The Controller observed. "Anything arising from the minutes of the last meeting? No? OK. Let's start with the current situation regarding websites... Raymond?"

"Little has changed from last week," began Ray Mingdon, Section Head for Internet Cryptanalysis. "We're still monitoring the movements of young Moslems who might try to fight in Syria. Eighteen more websites recruiting English Moslems to join the Islamic State Jihad have been closed down. We're still trying to find their sources. But as you know, no sooner have we closed one down than another springs up. So the crusade… erm… sorry poor choice of words… I mean the search goes on."

"Thank you Raymond. Josephine?" The Controller moved the meeting on.

"We are still monitoring our lads from the Syrian conflict. The files get thicker. I believe we are building a good case for the Crown Prosecution Service. This being so, why don't we take on all the returnees?"

"I believe that it is policy." The Controller explained, "All returnees will be tagged and put under house arrest. Except, of course, those we suspect of actually committing atrocities." He smiled round at the other members.

"I am referring," Clarified Jo Pullen, "To those who even now languish in our prisons."

"Oh I see," the Controller sighed. "Haven't we discussed this before? I'll make a note of your suggestion, but manpower will be the issue, as it always is. How will you deal with the increased number of suspects?"

"We would only need another analyst."

"As I said," The Controller observed. "Manpower might be the deciding factor."

"The second thing I want to bring to your attention," Jo continued quickly, "is the fact that Lord Kabir visited one of our boys, so I want to put him under surveillance."

"Lord Leyton?" The Controller looked surprised.

"That's right. We believe a new jamming device was used during his visit. Our departmental techie, Tom Canning, could not break it."

"OK. But, and I mean this, only minimum surveillance. I don't want him to know we are monitoring him. He's the highest profile Moslem we have in government and we don't want him screaming about a witch hunt."

"Understood, Controller."

"Tell your techie… Tom isn't it?" She nodded. "Tell Tom to send his material to Computer Intelligence." The Controller decided. "See if they can make head or tail of your mysterious jamming device."

The meeting continued for another three quarters of an hour. Although Jo was pleased to have made her points, she still felt frustrated. It seemed to her that the Controller was not really grasping her request to monitor all returnees. The longer the early ones remained in solitary, the stronger was their lack of co-operation. Also the more their mental health would be affected. Then the less likelihood of getting a clear conviction that the Crown Prosecution would be seeking.

Josephine Pullen returned to her department. She had underestimated the difficulties in moving to MI5. Despite the more recent Bond films showing a female Controller, there were still very few female department heads. That being the case she felt as though those round the table patronised her.
Putting the perceived frustration behind her, Jo wondered just how she was going to monitor a Lord of the Realm without ruffling feathers. They were even more chauvinistic than the Secret Service.

8.

Tariq spent most of the morning composing a letter to his visitor. As soon as the other man had spoken Tariq knew he was a Saudi. All Gulf Arabs seemed to exude an aloof superiority, but the Saudis were the worst. He had met several while fighting against the Iraqi army for The Islamic State. So he felt that he knew the recipient.

He sealed it in an envelope, but wrote nothing on the outside. He returned to re-reading the Holy Book. This was the second translation of the Quran he was using since his house arrest. Each English translation lost something of the original Arabic which focussed his mind. He was trying to immerse himself in as many translations as he could. He must be ready to meet Allah at whatever time. Then looked up in surprise when his brother coughed.

"Tariq?" Waleed asked, "What are you doing?"
"My little brother. How are you?"
"Good. Yeh. Good."
"I read the Quran. What more can a good Moslem do?" He arose from the bed and embraced the younger man. While they were close, Tariq signalled that he wanted to talk.
"You look pale, brother." Waheed spoke clearly. "You need some fresh air in the garden. I will tell the family, and then you won't be breaking any rules."
They smiled at each other while playing out this little charade in case the security were listening. Waheed went downstairs first. Tariq followed a few moments later. He respectfully kissed his mother's forehead while passing through the kitchen.
Tariq stepped into the sunshine. He screwed up his eyes against the glare. Waheed was sitting on a plank of wood supported by half a dozen breeze blocks under the only tree in the garden. Tariq waved him into the middle of the lawn. He was well aware that British Intelligence might hide microphones in place where they might talk.

"Yesterday a man visited me," the detainee began.

"The politician?"

"No. A Saudi. He told me that there is going to be some action soon."

"Wonderful news. What are we going to do?"

"I know nothing," Tariq admitted. "But you must meet this Saudi on Friday at Zuhr Prayers in Brixton Mosque. Give him this letter. See if you can get a contact number so I can talk to him directly."

"Of course." Waheed took the envelope. "Can I come with you this time?"

"If he says so. If you still want it. You can take your chance of becoming a martyr."

"Al-hum-dull-Allah. Thanks be to Allah, the Merciful."

9.

When Jasmine opened the gate there was someone in the back yard.

"Good afternoon Mr Robbins."

"Ohh!" A plump balding man spun round clutching a wire basket to his chest. "You nearly gave me 'eart attack."

"Sorry Mr Robbins."

"That's OK. Good afternoon Jasmine. You're looking as pretty as a picture."

"Thank you kind sir. But I don't feel it. It has been a long, hot day at school. Really boring. You know?"

"Yes I'm sure. I think our Darren's upstairs."

"He should be. The sixth form can leave whenever they don't have classes."

"You'll be there soon enough. Don't wish your life away. Got to get back now. See you later."

He held the door open for the schoolgirl to enter. She began to climb the stairs. He strode down the corridor towards the café at the front of the building.

Darren was doing his homework as she entered. He had his headset on, listening to music. She crept up behind him and put her hands over his eyes. Then leant down to whisper in his ear.
"Guess who?"

She felt his body freeze; goose-bumps appeared on his neck. Then he relaxed and began to quiver. He said nothing, but slowly stood. Her hands were still round his eyes. He was taller than her. As he slowly turned, he was caught in her embrace. They stood close together, but not touching.
His lips pressed against hers, then she did something she had never done before, she opened her teeth. His tongue flicked into her mouth. It was as though she had received an electric shock. She pushed her tongue in his mouth. Their bodies pressed together. Then they overbalanced and fell across the bed.
Before they knew what was happening her shirt was unbuttoned and he was kissing her left breast. Again it was electrifying. She did nothing to stop him. Her skirt was lifted and he pressed his hand on her pubic bone. She lowered her hand to his flies and with some difficulty, uncurled his penis out of its hot, snug nest. It straightened and swelled and was hot and big, and suddenly his body juddered and his mouth moved away from hers as he groaned. She could feel the hot fluid dribbling across the back of her hand.

"Ohh!" He murmured. "Oh my God. I'm sorry. So sorry. We shouldn't have."

"No. Don't be sorry. It is natural. It's OK. It's OK."

"It was wonderful. You're an angel. But this is wrong. Oh my God! OMG!"

"Promise me something."

"Anything."

"Never come inside me. I must never get pregnant. My father would kill me. My brothers will kill you. That is a fact. Believe me. They will kill you. We must never go the whole way. Never ever. Promise me."

"I promise. I'm so sorry. Ohh… No one has ever done that for me."

"I should hope not," she laughed.

"I – I didn't mean…"

"I love you. It is natural. Don't be sorry."

"I love you too. We are so lucky."

They hugged each other tightly and kissed each other's eyes and noses and lips as the realisation of mutual love had to be shown and shared and revelled in.

10.

The burgundy Bentley swooped down Marine Way towards The Strand in Brighton Marina. Suleiman pulled up by the barred gates into the yacht basin. A security guard slid open the bolts and pulled the gates open. The limousine purred down the slip road to rendezvous with 'Crescent Moon' – a Sunseeker, 34 metre yacht moored ready for embarkation. The chauffeur opened the back door. Four peers of the realm emerged. They were already chatty from champagne consumed on their journey from London.

Captain Abdulaziz ibn Awad and Chief Engineer Abdulrahman bin Nassr stood at the top of the gang plank to help the inebriated lords to board. Suleiman started unloading a hamper and two cardboard boxes of wine from the Bentley. Lord Anwar led his guests on a guided tour of his nautical realm. Rahman and Suleiman carried the supplies up the gangway. Aziz took them to their appropriate locations aboard.

Once out of earshot, Suleiman confirmed that Rahman would be picking up Imran Iqbal in Saint-Quay-Portrieux. Looking over both shoulders, the driver passed over a piece of paper with the rendezvous details on it. Then he retreated to the car. He had so much to do while his lordship was away. Then he had to be on time to meet the homecoming revellers.

Once everything was stowed, the captain entered the salon on the upper deck. Aziz uncorked a bottle of Krug Rose Champagne and began charging glasses. As soon as their guests emerged from the lower deck, they took a glass and raised them to their host.

"Here's to another successful campaign against fossil fuels."

There was laughter as the men quaffed happily. Aziz stood patiently beside Lord Anwar. Then his lordship turned and said,

"Saint Quay Port D'Armor Marina, if you please."

"Yes sir."

The ship's captain left the festivities and returned to the flybridge. He had already studied the charts so did not need to give them a second glance. He switched on the twin MTU 2435 16V 2000 engines. He waited for them to settle then pulled slowly away from the jetty.

He noticed the Bentley had already gone.

11.

Once back in her section, Jo checked each Intelligence Officer's Station. On reaching Faisal's she wanted an update.

"What have you found out about his lordship?"

"He is beyond reproach. A man of the people. Family migrated here after Partition in 1947. Neither parent spoke much English. They settled in Leyton."

"Hence his title."

"Yip. Hence his title. Dad became a taxi driver. Mum cooked samosas, selling to local shops and restaurants. Young Anwar attended the local secondary school. Got a scholarship to Manchester University. Studied IT. He became a computer programmer, then started his own company. He was a millionaire by the time he was twenty-five. A billionaire ten years later. Unlike any of his family, he became involved with the Conservative Party. A great advocate of Green Energy, sitting on several Commissions dealing with power. He is also very outspoken against extremism. He's often the government spokesman in all things radical Islam. He got his peerage for being a successful businessman and a campaigner for integrating Moslems into British Society."

"OK. That's why The Controller does not want to upset him."

"Well?"

"No. He's right. Let's play this one with kid gloves."

"We have several bases for observation." Faisal observed as he scrolled down the screen. "His Hampstead home. The House of Lords."

"Can't bug the Lords."

"Really?" Faisal laughed, "Imagine the Controller's face."

"Don't even suggest it."

"Each of four or five government committees. Suppose we can't bug those either."

"No."

"And a boat in Brighton Marina."

"A boat?"

"Yip," confirmed Faisal. "I believe he is on his way to France today."

"France?"

"He could be smuggling stuff in."

"Drugs? Alcohol? People?" Jo scratched her head. "There are too many possibilities with that one. OK. Let's start with a twenty-four-hour surveillance on his house."

"Follow him to work?"

"Yes. Just keep him under observation for the time being."

"We will need two vehicles and four Mobile Surveillance Officers," Faisal thought aloud. "Minimum. Two on at a time. Maybe a friendly neighbour would rent us a room overlooking his home."

"What? In Hampstead?" Jo asked incredulously.

"I'll see if the local bobbies can help us out on that one. They might have a safe house."

"Remember. Low-key. We don't want to involve the local constabulary. There could be a leak. Papers could find out."

"OK boss," Faisal finalised. "I'll get onto it right away. We'll start on Monday."

"Pity it can't be earlier."

"Yes." Faisal could not keep the sarcasm out of his voice. "This is the British Security Service not the CIA in *Homeland*."

She snorted and straightened up. "Yeh. Well, just do yer best, Agent Khan, just do yer best," In a pseudo American accent.

12.

'Crescent Moon' pulled into the marina in Brittany, northern France. Abdulrahman tied both end lines to the corresponding metal hoops on the harbour wall. Then he rolled the companionway onto the quayside.

Lord Leyton and his guests emerged from the galley in jovial mood. They trotted down the gangplank and wended their chatty way along the jetty towards the unmanned security barriers. Strode to the mini-roundabout, crossed the road and entered the *Atypic Restaurant* on the esplanade at Nouveau Port, Saint-Quay-Portrieux on the right. The owner greeted Lord Anwar like a long-lost family member and ushered them upstairs to his usual table, in the shade on the roof terrace, with a commanding view of the marina. After such a welcome, the cheerful group sat in anticipation of a splendid fish meal for which the restaurant was renowned.

As soon as the peers had disembarked, Abdulaziz secured the berth then cleared the galley. At the same time, Abdulrahman vacuumed the galley and companionway ready for their guests' return.

Once everything was ready, Rahman left the ship with a small 'Crescent Moon' rucksack on his back. On passing the *Atypic*, he could hear Lord Anwar's raucous laugh ringing out from the balcony. He knew they would not be able to see him as he passed. Even if they did, he was just another marina worker in blue overalls.

He walked on to the end of the harbour, but instead of turning left into the town, he crossed the road and wandered into the caravan park on the right. He soon found the rather nondescript Swift 590 RL Lifestyle 4-berth, parked in the middle, amid several similar looking mobile-homes.

Abdulrahman knocked on the door. He waited five seconds and knocked again. Then disappeared inside. The dull orange curtains gave it an eerie sunset glow. Rahman squinted in the surreal light. Three men sat at the table. They froze in mid-card game. Playing cards were scattered across the table top. They stared at him as though he were a leper.

"As-salaam alaykum," He greeted them.

"Wa alaykumu s-salaam," They politely replied but their eyes were still hostile.

It was easy to spot Imran Iqbal, tall and thin, with a magnificent black beard. The Syrian bomb maker was on the American CIA's most wanted list. His voice was quiet but commanding. Rahman pulled a pair of blue overalls from his rucksack. Imran gathered them and disappeared into the toilet. Rahman sat with the Algerian drivers to wait. They were not very chatty. He found north African Arabs unfriendly. They were too serious. But he was not here to socialise so accepted their hostility.

Fifteen minutes later Rahman emerged from the motor caravan. He was followed by Imran, also wearing the ubiquitous blue overalls with the 'Crescent Moon' logo on his chest. He was carrying the backpack. If anyone had noticed they might have observed that it was heavier than on the outward journey. They strode along the quayside, past the restaurant and through the barriers.

Once aboard, the newcomer was immediately taken to the lower deck. They entered one of the smaller guest bedrooms. Aziz pulled aside a sliding panel. It revealed a tiny hidden cabin in the mid-starboard side. It was just big enough for a narrow bunk and built-in locker. It did not have a porthole. It had a low-wattage bulb in the sloping ceiling. Aziz secured the 'door' and checked that no light escaped the entrance section. Once satisfied, the ship's crew returned to the upper decks, ready to set sail as soon as their guests returned.

13.

Suleiman emerged from Brixton tube station, turned right past *WH Smith's* and along Brixton Road. He was dressed in a long dark overcoat despite the warm weather, with a lacy white Moslem skull cap squarely on his head. The Saudi went passed the shops and under the twin rail bridges that have dominated the high street since Victorian times.

He reached the first major right-hand junction where two roads joined Brixton Road. One had been blocked off, creating a banjo cul-de-sac. Two police vans were parked on double yellow lines. He wandered across this space onto Gresham Road. After about a hundred metres he came to the Brixton Mosque on the left. It was in an ordinary detached house next to another that was home to 'Choice Tutors', a private crammer school.

It was nearly quarter to one and Zuhr Prayer was due to start. Suleiman removed his shoes and walked up the steps into the prayer room. It was already quite full. He went through into the washroom, sprinkled water on his socks and hands; then splashed his face; he touched his mouth, nostrils, ear-holes and eyes, with wet fingers. He was cleansed for prayer. He took his place near the door and stood facing Mecca. Suleiman kowtowed on the threadbare carpet, to begin his preparation for prayer.

After 'midday' prayer, most of the congregation found their shoes and left by the front door. A number made their way upstairs to the meeting rooms and school. Suleiman followed them. He went into one of the smaller rooms. It had a small table surrounded by four hard backed chairs. He also saw two men turn towards him. He introduced himself to Waheed Siddiqi and asked how his brother was. Waheed handed him Tariq's letter. Then he introduced him to Nazir Bashirn. Suleiman asked him about his cousin Khalid.
Then the three men settled round the table. Suleiman opened the letter. He read the contents then slid it into his inner pocket.

The Saudi explained that he was in the last stages of planning an attack on England. It had taken over two years to place the personnel required and store the equipment needed. He admitted having enough fighters. But many of the more experienced ones, like Tariq and Khalid were under house arrest. Not only were they tagged, but their homes were bugged so direct contact was impossible. That was why he was settling up these liaisons with contacts of the main fighters. He asked Nazir to act as the contact with his cousin Khalid Ahmad. And he confirmed that Waleed was the link to Tariq. He emphasised that they must discuss nothing with their families within their own homes.

Suleiman gave each of them a mobile phone and a packet of SIM cards. He emphasised that they were only to be used in an emergency. They had to keep their messages short. Also, the SIM card had to be destroyed immediately after use. They vowed that they would never use a SIM card more than once. They also vowed that their destruction was imperative so the British Secret Service could not trace them. He stressed that each SIM card would link to his phone. All these cards had been doctored so that Suleiman could communicate directly with them. But they would issue a different signature when the Security Services tried to monitor them. That was key to them not being traced.

He promised to keep in touch at Friday Zuhr Prayer in Brixton Mosque. Suleiman also said that he would text them on these phones should there be an emergency. They had to be ready to move quickly. As most of the recruits were under observation, the authorities might discover something unexpectedly. In that case he might have to bring their plans forward. So they had to be ready to move immediately.

Suleiman stood. He asked them to give him five minutes head start before leaving the mosque. The Pakistani-British agreed as the Saudi walked out of the door. They put their new phones away and discussed where they could dispose of the used SIM. Nazir thought they could only make them unserviceable if they were cut. It was imperative that they tear them into little pieces and the bits scattered. After about five minutes they too went downstairs and out of the front door.

14.

An hour later, Waheed and Nazir visited the Ahmad family. They chatted amicably to Khalid's father about the expense of children's university education in the UK. His pet topic was the price of food in London. He reminded them about the price of food in Pakistan when he was a boy. After a small glass of Qehwa – green tea with cardamom – they went into the garden for a cigarette. As devout Moslems, neither of them actually smoked, but it was an excuse to leave the house without raising listener's eyebrows. Having heard the conversations downstairs Khalid joined them.

After the initial greetings he got straight to the point.
"How is Tariq?"
"He is reading the Quran." Waheed reported.
"I tried that, but I haven't got his piety."
"He says for you to be patient." Waheed said.

"Yes," Khalid laughed, "He knows me very well. For three years we were in Iraq. Then later Syria. We were like brothers. Brothers in arms. Fighting and killing together. Not brothers from the same woman."

Waleed tried to recall what the Saudi said, "You may not have to wait long. If there is a breach of security, they may bring the attack forward. Be patient. Also," Waheed added after a short pause, "Tariq said for you to keep fit. You must be ready when the time comes."

"Yes. Tariq is right. Nazir?"

"Yes cousin."

"Can you get hold of an exercise bike or rowing machine?"

"I will ask round the family. I'm sure someone will have something. Especially when they know it is for you."

"Give my good wishes to Tariq. Tell him I am being patient. I am exercising and I am waiting for the call."

Shaking hands with his visitor, he returned to the house. He knew he should not be seen talking to groups of men. The tag monitors him when he was not in his room.

Khalid felt strangely elated having spoken to somebody from outside his family. He cleared some space and begin an exercise regime. He needed to be in top condition to face the next challenge. Action at last!

15.

When Jazz arrived home, she knew something was wrong. Her father was standing in front of the empty fireplace looking very serious. Her mother was sitting on the sofa and it looked as though she had been crying.

"Jasmine, my lovely daughter," Ali began formally. "You will be sixteen soon."

"Next month, Papa."

"Yes. You are my youngest child. You are the diamond in your mother's eye. You have brought us such joy."

"Thank you, Papa." She smiled at her mother, but got no response.

"It is time for you to get married."

"Papa!" Jasmine screamed. "I must finish my education. I want to be a doctor. I want to bring pride on my family."

"Hush, hush my child." Ali calmed her, "You have brought great pride. Great joy. Believe me. Your mother and I are proud of you. But you know our customs. When I left Mirpur in Azad Kashmir I had nothing. I promised my very good friend that if I had a daughter and he had a son, then they would be married. He gave me the money to come to this country."

"Papa..."

"Hush. Your father is speaking," he said rather pompously. "I had wonderful news from him. He has a son. His name is Muhammed Akbar Khan. He is now eighteen. He wants to marry you... so... next month you and your mother will return to Pakistan to get married."

"Papa. Please. I do not know him. Maybe he is ugly."

"Silly girl," her father laughed knowingly. "Beauty is in the eye of the beholder. You know that. Com'on now. Give me a hug. Your papa is making you a good life."

"Mama. Please, I do not love him."

"I did not meet your papa before we got married," her mother reminded her. "And look how good our life has been. Now be an obedient girl. Do as your father desires. It is your duty to the family."

"Mama but... I love someone else."

"What is the stupid girl talking about?" Ali looked at his wife for help.

"I love Darren," Jasmine declared.

"Darren!" Ali was perplexed. "It isn't a Pakistani name."

"He is English. He is a sixth-former at my school and..."

"Is he a Moslem?" Ali's voice was rising.

"No... but he's..." Jasmine's voice broke with emotion.

"I forbid it." Ali proclaimed. "You will marry a Moslem. You will forget the Infidel immediately. I forbid you to ever see him again. You will do what I say," he turned to his wife, "I told you no good would come from co-education. No good I told you. Girls should go to a girl's school so they do not get these silly ideas. It is not natural I tell you. It is.. it is Un-Islamic."

"I will never be happy again. All my dreams are destroyed."

"Don't be a diva Jazz," Ali reasoned. "You will have a good life with Muhammed..."

"Has he got two legs?" Jasmine asked unnecessarily.

"Don't be facetious to your father. Now go to your room and get ready for the best day in your life."

She ran from the room snivelling. They heard her sobs for several hours that evening.

16.

Abdulaziz steered the 'Crescent Moon' gently towards the disembarkation jetty. Abdulrahman held the mooring rope in his right hand, swinging it gently. Suleiman was waiting to catch the rope. In the galley four lords were

34

howling with laughter, oblivious of the preparations for their smooth transition from the sea to the land.

Rahman tossed the rope high. It arched though the air and was ably caught by the waiting chauffeur. He pulled it tight and deftly looped it round the bollard. Then he moved towards the rear of the boat in time to catch the second line. This too was secured to the jetty. At that point Rahman rolled out the gangplank. Suleiman strode up to meet him. The ship's engineer nodded and smiled vigorously,
"He has no luggage!"
He declared and passed over two holdalls which were quickly transferred to the waiting car. Suleiman understood that Imran was aboard. Two boxes and a hamper were passed down. Meanwhile, Aziz left the cockpit and went to wait in the galley.

Finally the four Members of Parliament wandered off the ship and into the waiting limousine. Suleiman silently closed the rear door. Then opened the driver's door. He secured the seat belt and then tapped the starting button.
The luxurious automobile silently glided up the slope and out of the marina. At the same time, Abdulrahman untied the restraining lines and stepped aboard. He pulled the gangway up after him. Abdulaziz eased the vessel towards the main moorings ready for closing down for the night.

17.

Two white vans were in the converted garage area of the stables block. All three occupants of the stately home were busy on the vehicles. Little sounds could be heard inside the workshop: the clink of a tool on metal, the clatter when one is dropped and the human 'humph' when exertion was required.

Ibrahim lifted the rear seat unit out of the van and placed it on the workbench between the vehicles. Hussain put the base plate for the jack mechanism into the empty space. Ibrahim measured out the dimensions on the van floor. He used a black felt pen to show exactly where the bolts had to be placed. Hussain used a heavy-duty drill to make the holes, careful not to go too deep and accidently drill into fittings under the chassis. Then Ibrahim pulled the plate in place. As the van was over the work pit, it was easy for Hussain to push the first bolt through the hole and hold it steady with a ring spanner.

"OK." He shouted,

Ibrahim finger-tightened the nut, careful not to cross the threads. He then used an electric wrench, with a box spanner attachment, to tighten it. Once all four were secure, the men went towards a tarpaulin covered shape at the back of the garage.

"Naveed," Hussain shouted. "Can you help us lift this roof jack?"

The chief mechanic placed his screwdriver and wiped his hands on his overalls.

"Are you ready?" He seemed surprised.

"This is the fifth van. We get quicker the more we do."

The jack was on a wheeled pallet, so they easily manhandled it to the rear of the truck. Then all three struggled to lift it into the space. The tricky bit came when they had to lift the mechanism onto the shaped base plate now bolted firmly to the floor. But as with the previous vans, they eventually secured the retaining bolts to make sure it was placed precisely.

Now Hussain brought the roof panel across. He manhandled it over the gaping hole where it had once sat. Ibrahim began to raise the jack using wheeled handles. Once it reached its maximum height Hussain lowered the face mask then lit the oxy-acetylene welder. He deftly joined the roof to the clamp. His co-mechanic pushed the rubber trim in place right round the outside of roof section so it would make a watertight seal when realigned with the van top.

When Ibrahim reversed the jack mechanism, the roof slowly settled in place. The rubber seal settling exactly where it should, making a rainproof joint. Lastly Hussain introduced a split-pin rod to secure the hinges at the back. Next time the roof was raised only the front would move upwards.

Now it was assembled, Naveed brought over the hinged firing-plate flaps which had to be attached to the rear of the roof tubes. These four components were welded in place by Hussain. Again Ibrahim checked them to make sure they opened and closed efficiently. Naveed returned to the work bench and retrieved four lids which were then screwed to the front of the roof tubes. To all intents and purposes the vehicle had four tubular storage units attached to its roof. Often used by plumbers to store long copper pipes.

While they were busy, Ibrahim picked up one of the now redundant seats. He carried it across the quad and into the 'stables' on the north side on the square. He pulled open the doors.

Three more vans were housed here. They had their jacks attached and quadruple tubes installed. They had also been resprayed, which gave them a more acceptable appearance. He placed the seat on the pile of other attachments that had been removed from the vehicles. There was just enough room for seven completed vans in the garage.

At least, that was the target.

18.

As soon as the boat was moored, Abdulaziz went below to the secret cabin. He knocked on the panelling and told the

38

occupant who he was. Many years of warfare had left Aziz very wary of the warrior class. They were often armed and would over-react in self-defence if awakened too abruptly. When there was an answering response, Aziz pulled back the secret door.

Imran emerged from the niche. Then he followed the captain upstairs to the toilet. He later joined them in the cockpit. He breathed in the fresh air, deeply.

"You did not have any luggage?" queried Abdulrahman.

"No," answered their guest. "Serving Allah does not need material things. I always travel light. It protects my identity... and my movements from the infidels."

"Fair enough." Rahman understood, "We will be taking you to a safe house tonight. Then tomorrow you will be taken to Gayhurst Manor."

"Allah willing," intoned the holy man.

"Inshallah," echoed the crew.

Three men in blue overalls left the ship and trundled along the jetty. They passed through the security gates and onto the North Wall Promenade, before cutting through to The Strand. They walked between two rows of four-storey buildings until they came to the safe house. It was at the end of the block.

Aziz opened the ground floor door and they entered the luxuriously appointed lounge. Rahman went to the kitchen area to fill the kettle and a saucepan ready to boil some rice.

"You can have the first bedroom upstairs," Abdulaziz directed. "Rahman will cook something. Then you can sleep until the morning. Another man, Hussain Ahmed, will pick you up tomorrow."

"I understand. Will you sleep here?"

"No. We stay on the ship. Better security."

"I understand. I will wait 'til tomorrow for Hussain."

Imran went upstairs to find his sleeping quarters. He wondered if he would be able to sleep. Just as he had done in the secret cabin, he pulled the duvet and pillow onto the floor. That was where he planned to sleep.

By the time he got downstairs, Aziz had laid the table. Rahman handed him a mug of Gulabi Chai – a pink milky tea – and returned to preparing a chicken biryani on Basmati Rice. He sprinkled saffron into the rice, giving it a satisfying pale yellow colour. Once it was on the table, the mariners left the Syrian alone with his thoughts, until the morning.

19.

Tom Canning took Faisal's recording to Computer Intelligence on the top floor. They boasted the best, state of the art surveillance equipment, outside GCHQ at Cheltenham. Although the Upper Management Team encouraged everyone to familiarise themselves with other departments, because of the highly sensitive nature of the material each department had to handle, they were not welcoming. This section was no different. Tom felt a little lost.

"Can I help you?" Tom read 'Roger Banter' on his name badge.

"Hi Roger. I'm Tom Canning." He pointed helpfully at his own badge. "My Section Chief told me to bring this here." And he held up a memory stick.

"What is it?" Roger asked, rather disdainfully.

"It is the recording of someone we have under surveillance. They appear to be using a new kind of jamming device."

"New kind of jamming device?" His interest was aroused. "Did you use our software to cancel the jammer?"

"Yes. But to no avail."

"That's interesting." But he did not put his hand out,

"In fact the sound is most unusual."

"Is it now?" Tom noticed that his hand moved towards him,

"Move like a cacophony of sound. A blending of huge amounts of sound, Not just scrambled sound."

Roger Banter held out his hand, despite his determination not to.

"Can you leave this with us?"

"Of course. We have recorded a small section where the subject is talking, then the device cuts in. We would like you to descramble the conversation for us."

Roger took the device. He looked at it then wrote something in a ledger. Once satisfied, he turned the book to Tom. The memory-stick's serial number had been recoded. Tom signed on the dotted line then asked,
"How long will it take?" There was an intake of breath,
"How long is a piece of string? Look," and he glanced at the name badge. "Erm... Look Tom if this is what you say it is... if this is a new jamming signal it might take some time to decipher. I'll let you know how we are getting along on Monday. OK?"
"My Section Head was hoping it might be sooner."
"Sorry. No one works at weekends these days. I'll put it into the Decode Breaker over the weekend. We should have an answer by Monday. Fingers crossed."

He gestured the same, turned and disappeared through frosted glass doors. Tom wandered out of the departmental reception and back to the security of the place where he worked.

20.

Suleiman pulled into Pall Mall and drove sedately along the historic street. He stopped outside the Reform Club. Thomas, the doorman, rushed to open the rear door before the chauffeur could move. Five lords-a-laughing tumbled out of the Bentley. They followed the club official into the hallowed interior. He had elaborately waved the car door closed, like a magician's hand over a top hat.

Suleiman waited until he was sure Lord Anwar would not rush down the steps with further instructions. Then drove towards Trafalgar Square. He pulled over as soon as he could. Suleiman took an iPhone from the glove compartment. He opened it. Then slid a new SIM card into the empty recess. He dialled the number of Gayhurst Manor.

"Naveed?"

"Speaking."

"Your friend arrived today as planned." The driver informed him.

"Good news. Then everything is ready."

"Hussain must pick him up from the safe-house tomorrow morning."

"He can't. We are going to Docklands City auctions. Hussain will be required to drive one of the vans."

"How many vans do you still need?"

"Two."

"Well, you and Ibrahim could drive them back. But Hussain will need the Land Cruiser."

"OK." Naveed thought of an alternative. "We will take the early train to London."

"Then get the train to Surrey Quays. It is not far from the auction house."

"OK. Hussain can drop us at Northampton station. Then he can go to Brighton for you."

"Good." Suleiman sounded relieved. "Will they be the last vans?"

"Yes. Once we have these two, it will only take a week or so to change them."

"Al-hamdulillah," Suleiman praised Allah. "I'll call when I have any more news."

"I understand. Masallam." Naveed signed off.

"Masallamah."

Suleiman turned off the mobile phone. He slipped the casing apart and took out the SIM card. He tucked it into his left-hand pocket to be shredded later. He returned the phone to the glove compartment. Two minutes later, the Bentley pulled into the evening traffic and moved across London to his lordship's Hampstead address.

As he neared the three-metre high brick façade, the chauffeur pushed a button on the dashboard. The substantial oaken gates slowly swept open in a gentle open-armed gesture of welcome. He swung into the yawning space in front of the garage and pressed another button. In response the garage door rolled up to reveal a well-lit interior. He pulled between two parked cars. He pressed the buttons again and the garage door, as well as the gate, closed to secure the compound.

Suleiman walked from the garage, straight into the kitchen area. He peered in the fridge and saw his plated salad. It was sealed in cling-film, like an advert for healthy eating.

He took it and a bottle of still water to his bedroom. This was in the male servants' quarters, in the basement of this rambling four-storey structure.

21.

Saturday is always busy at Docklands City 2020 auction house. It opens at 09:00 for punters to look over the vehicles and the sale starts promptly at 13:00. They are renowned as auctioneers to H.M. Customs & Excise, independent bailiffs, local authorities and the police. Their vehicles have high mileages, but are usually maintained to the highest level. This is what Naveed is looking for. He also knows that they had just been through a stringent MOT, so are as ready as possible for the road. After all, he does not need them to last for years, just a few weeks of trouble-free motoring.

It was raining quite heavily as Hussain drove Naveed and Ibrahim to Northampton station. They were scheduled to catch the 06:18 train for Euston, London. By the time their train arrived, the rain had cleared, but the day remained overcast, with the menace of rain.

From Euston, they caught the tube to Highbury & Islington. Then the London Overground to Surrey Quays, arriving at 08:24. Naveed led them out of the suburban red-brick station into the grey drizzle. They turned left along Lower Street passed many small shops. As it was still raining and over half an hour to the auction house opening, they stopped at a small café. Ibrahim ordered two black teas and they prepared to wait.

An hour later, the rain had eased enough for them to make their way to the auction rooms. They took their time closely examining all the medium sized vans; checking MOTs, tax-disc history, maintenance record and ownership papers. By midday Naveed had earmarked five or six possibilities. He also had twenty-five thousand pounds in fifty-pound notes arranged in bundles of £5,000. These were distributed in different pockets, so he was particularly nervous. The limit they set themselves was ten thousand pounds for either vehicle. That was about what he paid for the others. The extra five was in case they ran over slightly. But he was warned not to use it up on the first vehicle.

However, he was well aware that time was running out. He was determined that the vehicles were not going to be the reason why they could not complete the project.

22.

As soon as Hussain dropped his two colleagues at the station, he put the Brighton Marina postcode into his sat nav and waited for satellite connection. The window wipers of the white Land Cruiser occasionally swished across the windscreen removing the intermittent silver raindrops. He daydreamed of the time when England would be a caliphate and everyone would follow sharia law. Every good Moslem dreamt of this moment; to live in the perfect Islamic State where the Quran was followed by everyone. He could not understand why Moslem clerics in England spoke out against ISIS. They kept saying that Islam was a peaceful religion, but Mohammed The Prophet, peace be upon him, had shown them the way. Indeed The Prophet had taken up the sword against Jews and Christians indeed all non-believers. In fact, Mohammed the Prophet had been the first caliph.

Hussain simply could not understand why English Moslems denied their religious heritage. It simply consolidated his belief that they were bad Moslems. They deserved to die with the other kaffars.

"Drive 200 metres and turn right. Turn right."

The expressionless male sat nav voice broke into his reverie. Hussain checked his mirror, touched the accelerator and pulled the Land Cruiser into the traffic. He allowed the sat nav to direct him through the confusing maze of streets towards the city limits.

After a short time, he was on the A508 heading south through the leafy suburbs of Northampton. He crossed the flyover at Delapre Wood. Then he joined a faster dual-carriageway, the A45 until it joined the M1 South at junction 15. Once on the motorway he brought the four-litre engine up to 70 miles an hour and touched the cruise button. He had no intention of being picked up for speeding. He adjusted the window wipers for less frequent sweeps then glanced at the sat nav. Just over two hours before he would arrive in Brighton. Pushing the play button Hussain relaxed as he listened to recordings of readings from the Quran, sometimes joining in with passages that he knew by heart. And he knew quite a lot. It was good to have the time to practice reading. It was good to have the time to quiz himself on the Holy Book.

Listening to the Quran always brought him peace.

23.

Suleiman Al Dossari woke to the prayer call on his alarm clock. His mother had bought it for him in Mecca, as a 'thank you gift' when he chaperoned her and his three sisters on Umrah, a pilgrimage to the Holy City outside the Hajj period.

Sleepily, he pulled on a white thobe and wandered to the bathroom. One of the off-duty security officers was washing his feet. Suleiman washed his ears, mouth and nose, and snorted mucus from his throat noisily, cleansing himself thoroughly before prayer. Then he splashed water on his feet and hands. Once clean, he plodded up the back stairs to the prayer room on the second floor for the Fajr, or predawn prayer. He took his place on the mat with the gardener and three security officers. Unbid, as was his habit, Al Dossari led the prayer.

The Anwar household tried to maintain a traditional Pakistani-Moslem ethos. This was partly due to the fact that Lord Kabir's mother lived with them, and as the matriarch of the family she influenced it greatly. Ever since her husband died, she had lived with her eldest child, as was customary in her homeland. She and Lady Leyton took her two granddaughters and the female maids into the room adjoining the men's prayer room. It was equipped with one-way glass, framed by lace curtains, so they could see the Imam and hear his preaching, but none of the men could spy on them at prayer.

Suleiman returned to his quarters and dozed for an hour until the second prayer at sunrise. This time, he dressed in his uniform: a single-breasted black suit and matching tie.

After prayer, he had breakfast in the servants' dining room. Again it was sparsely attended. Three security guards were sharing a hummus dip. The chef made fresh chapattis every morning and they were good when eating dips, which he prepared the day before. Today the Saudi helped himself to two hard boiled eggs and slices of white bread. He also drank black coffee.

Today being a Saturday meant that his lordship would not be attending any committees, or the House of Lords. But today, was different and it would be another two or three hours before the chauffeur need return to the Reform Club.

24.

Jasmine stayed in her bedroom the next morning. Although she texted several friends she did not mention the arranged marriage to anybody. She wanted to get her mind round her options before she told anyone anything. There was always a chance that one of her friends might inform her family of her depression, if they were genuinely concerned for her mental state, and she did not want her family forewarned of her intentions.

It was a dismal wet morning that matched her mood perfectly. Normally a light-hearted, jolly person she felt a physical pain in her chest. She could actually feel her heart breaking. It was a deep, deep pain right in the core of her chest. Although, she could not see a way out of her present predicament, there was no way she was going to Pakistan to marry a total stranger. It was all so unfair. All her dreams were shattered like a smashed mirror. Hurtful splintered shards glinting up at her through her tears. Everything she had known was gone. All the certainty of her childhood, all the things she took for granted about her family, her parent's love and support, her security and her future… all destroyed.

At ten she took a shower and got dressed. She could not face her mother or food so avoided the kitchen. She slinked out the back way. It did not cross her mind that her escape was all too easy. The things she had said the previous night. Had her apparent disobedience gone unnoticed? Ali was incandescent with rage. None of his children had ever refused his wishes. He was not going to change his plans for an adolescent girl who thought she was in love.

So Ali charged Waheed to keep an eye on her. He no longer trusted his own daughter. Seconds after she left the back yard, her older brother slipped out behind her.

Although she was wearing a black headscarf, like so many girls on the streets of Brixton, her bright red umbrella was like a torch blazoning the way for Waheed. Also, because she was carrying an umbrella, it was easier for him to see when she was turning so he could avoid visual detection. When she stopped to look in the shop window, before ducking into the alleyway, her sibling was tying his shoe laces behind a conveniently parked car.

As soon as she disappeared into the passageway, Waheed sprinted across the road. He dodged into the narrow entranceway. She was nowhere to be seen. He ran to the end of the alley and peeped to the left. Nothing to be seen. Then right. A red umbrella was disappearing through a green gate. He moved quickly down the dark brick alley. As he reached out to the gate, he heard a door shut. He pushed the gate open and squeezed through the aperture. Again she was not visible. He trotted to the back door and opened it carefully. He could hear noises from the café. He was just about to turn away, when he heard his sister's crying. He crept inside the building followed the sound, upstairs.

When Jasmine had entered Darren's room he immediately knew something was terribly wrong.
"Hey. What's up Jazzie?"
He stood and she lurched forward into his arms and began to sob, quietly at first.
"Hey, hey." He led her to the bed. "It can't be that bad. Sit down and…"

But he was unable to finish the sentence. She had collapsed across the bed on top of him, her body convulsing in spasms of grief. Darren uttered consoling noises, but was unable to understand why she was so upset. He began kissing her face, tasting the saltiness of her tears as they splashed onto his upturned face.

He did not notice Waheed looking at them through the crack in the door. He did not hear the sharp intake of breath as the voyeur saw his sister lying across a bed with a strange male. A non-Moslem! He did not feel the man tiptoe downstairs. He did not see him rush out into the back yard to vomit up his breakfast behind the dustbins.

25.

Suleiman drove across London at about ten to pick up Lord Anwar from the Reform Club. His lordship was in a good mood. He usually was after staying at the club with his cronies. As it was Saturday he planned to spend some time at his family home in Hampstead. He had a speech to write about the alternative energy bill in the House of Lords on Monday afternoon. That being the case, he dismissed his chauffeur for the rest of the day.

Al Dossari took the Bentley to the rear of the garage and began cleaning it. First vacuuming and polishing the inside, then washing and buffing the bodywork. He took a pride in the appearance of the luxury limousine, because he knew it was important for the prestige and status of the owner. Fundamentally he did not regard this as important in life, but as a cover for his role as a driver for a member of the aristocracy, it was important for his own protection.

26.

Hussain Ahmed drove as close to the house as possible. Then walked round to the bollard barrier and inserted his key. The pillar sank into the paving stones. He jumped back into the Land Cruiser and reversed into the private slot. Because mobile phones were so easily tracked by British security forces, he had not made any contact with the man he was about to pick up.

Having come across war veterans before, he was careful not to approach too silently. He rang the doorbell and rapped out a tattoo on the knocker. After a couple of seconds he slid the Yale key into the lock. The door yawned open.

"Salaam," he called through the opening. "It is only..."

He was grabbed from behind and held in a painful headlock. Unable to speak, Hussain tapped submissively on the arm holding a vice like grip round his throat. He heard the door slam shut behind them and then he was sent staggering across the room. He ended up against the breakfast bar. He massaged his throat and turned to meet his aggressor.

Imran Iqbal stood almost two metres high with a large, black bushy beard. He was dressed in a long white and grey stripped kaftan with a small white Moslem skull cap. But it was not the long carving knife centimetres from his throat that held Hussain's attention. It was the piercing black eyes. They seemed to glow, boring into its hapless prey. They were emotionless, like those of an eagle surveying its quarry. They stood like that for what felt like a long time. Then the eyes blinked and the lank body relaxed.

"Salaam Alaykum," he intoned in a rich baritone voice. "You are late."

"Alaykum Salam. I got here as soon as I could."

"Let's go. I've business to do here, in Brighton. We also have some equipment to pick up in Aldershot."

"OK. But you need to change. You must not… umm… not attract attention."

"Do you know Aldershot?"

"No worries. I'll use the GPS."

"We must be there at five o' clock."

Hussain glanced at his watch.

"We have plenty of time. Now we have to make you look like a businessman."

Imran nodded slowly. The driver returned to the van and brought in a large dark blue suitcase. Fifteen minutes later, Hussain drove the suited stranger with the big bushy beard into the town centre. He dropped him off in North Street and was told, in no uncertain terms, to return in one hour.

Sure enough, when Hussain slowed at the corner of North and Portland Street, Imran was waiting. The car had just stopped and the bearded stranger climbed into the rear. He was carrying two identical black attaché cases, which he placed on the seat beside him. Hussain pulled back into the impatient traffic, returning to the safe house. There were still three hours to wait before they could go to Aldershot, so they decided that it was safer to wait in Brighton then to find somewhere to wait when they got there.

It was imperative not to attract attention. A small mistake now could scupper months of planning. Hussain did not want to be the one to do that. Now Imran had his cases, he was much more relaxed to follow the other man's advice.

27.

Waheed arrived at Brixton Mosque a bit late for Zuhr Prayer. He joined the overspill congregation outside under a tarpaulin, stretched across the rear courtyard. As soon as the prayer had finished he hurried in order to walk home with his father.

Ali Siddiqi was a popular member of the mosque. He had been attending for over fifty years so he could not merely walk home. Ali spoke to many people about their problems and plans on the pavement outside. Waheed waited for him to be alone. If the old man was aware of his second son loitering, he did not show it. It was some time before they fell into step on the short journey home.

The younger man was not sure how to approach the delicate topic. It was not until they were within sight of their home before he blurted out his story. He briefly related how he had followed Jasmine to Darren's home. He dealt in graphic detail, seeing her lying on a bed with the Infidel.

The old man froze to the spot. His swarthy face drained of colour. First he was sweating.

"She has brought dishonour to our family."

Then a spasm shook his frail frame.

"She is spoilt. She is not pure. She cannot share a life with a good Moslem man any more. She is possessed with Satan. Satan is in her heart. The devil is in her soul. She is possessed with evil. Only her death can change this dishonour."

With a sinking heart the young man listened to his father's rambling logic. His emotions plummeted. Shock and anger were replaced with the humiliation of shame. Waheed could feel it spread, like an evil dark cloud, upon their family.

28.

Imran Iqbal had memorised the address in Aldershot. He gave Hussain the postcode who typed it into the sat nav. Once satellite connection was established, it informed them that it would take an hour and a half. They decided to leave Brighton at three thirty.

In order not to attract too much attention, they wore dark suits. Like all those who resided at Gayhurst Manor, Hussain had already shaved off his beard. Imran refused point blank to remove his facial hair. Hussain did not push the matter. Despite his huge bushy growth, he could pass in a cosmopolitan city like Brighton, as a professional consultant.

They followed the A23 as far as the London Orbital. Then followed the motorway until junction 10. Here, Hussain turned left along the A3 as far as Guildford, past the austere brick-built cathedral on the left, then up the hill, leaving the metropolis behind. Near the top of the hill they veered left into the looping right-hander onto the Hog's Back. The driver was careful to keep the Land Cruiser at the sixty mile-an-hour restriction for its entire length.

Hussain was taken by surprise when the sat nav announced;

"You have reached your destination on the left."

They were not in Aldershot, but still on the tail-end of the Hog's Back. Hussain put on the left hand indicator and stopped. The car stood in the blocked entrance of a layby. A tree had collapsed, cutting off all possible entry. He looked in confusion at Imran, who waved him forward.

"Go a bit further."

The exit to the layby was coned off. Again Hussain slowed. Imran slipped out and removed some of the 'police' cones. He waved Hussain backwards into the layby. Then replaced the cone barrier. The Land Cruiser disappeared behind the thick vegetation which surrounded the empty layby. It visually cut it off from the road. It was eerily quiet, screened from the busy highway.

"Are you sure this is the place?" asked the bemused driver.

"Come on," Imran encouraged him. "Let's open the back."

Hussain opened the rear doors. Imran gathered his cases. Hussain flattened the back seats. His accomplice placed the blue suitcase and one of the black attaché cases into the foot-space of the front passenger seat. He took the other black leather case with him. Imran moved east to look over the fallen tree that blocked the entrance to their layby from the westward flowing traffic.

Hussain moved in the opposite direction. In security training in the Yemen, he had been taught to cover all entrances, so moved west automatically. When he reached the end of the layby he could see the traffic yet remain concealed behind the tangle of branches and brambles that infested the layby edge. There was a convoy of army vehicles passing on the other side of the road, heading in an easterly direction. Being a peacetime column, it was not solid with army vehicles, but broken up with civilian cars, vans, busses and lorries, which had overtaken the military ones and got mixed up with them. He stayed hidden behind the foliage as the intermittent convoy of tank transporters rumbled past. He could feel the vibration in the tarmac under his feet as the heavy units thundered by.

Suddenly, one of the army personnel transporters swerved across the road. It veered straight into the layby, removing three cones in its path. A figure in jungle-camouflage uniform leapt out of the truck. He ran back to the cones, rearranging them to prevent any other vehicles from following them. Then beckoned to Hussain as he jog trotted after the army lorry.

Imran was chatting to a British army officer. He handed over the black attaché case. The officer opened it and Hussain could see that it was full of fifty pound notes. Imran gestured for him to help three British soldiers transferring their load. The truck contained some reinforced silver canisters. Hussain grabbed one cylinder from the guy in the truck. It was quite heavy and cold to the touch. It had the yellow and black hazardous material warning signs emblazoned across its side. He passed it to the uniform in his vehicle who stacked it. Then went back for another. The other soldier worked alternately with him.

They soon had twenty-eight containers neatly packed in the rear of the Land Cruiser. The soldiers tumbled aboard their truck. It roared as the driver began to execute a tight three-point turn. Hussain ran back to the cones. He only just managed to remove enough. The dark green vehicle angrily breathed out hot blue fumes, waiting for a gap in the traffic. It swayed several times as the driver balanced the throttle and the clutch. Then sped in a tight curve out of the layby. It disappeared eastward in hot pursuit of the convoy.

Then he heard the Land Cruiser start up. It stopped just outside the coned off area. Hussain replaced them and went to his vehicle. Imran had already moved over to the passenger seat. He climbed into the driving seat and typed in the co-ordinates for Gayhurst Manor. Once the satellite connection was made he eased into the traffic. Barely ten minutes had passed since they had entered the rendezvous point. There was no evidence that anything had taken place.

The following day, a team of road maintenance engineers removed the tree, wondering which transport department had coned it off.

29.

Suleiman searched the pockets of all his clothes. He wanted to destroy any evidence that might link him to the events now taking place. He shredded the old SIM cards. These were carefully collected in pieces into a tissue. They were less suspicious to dump later. Everyone put tissue into public waste baskets. No eyebrows raised. That was the aim.
The second phone was on the table. He slid back the receptacle. It looked clean. He inserted a new card. Then the phone actually rang. The Saudi nearly had a heart attack. It was so unexpected. He raised the phone to the side of his face.

"Yes?" He answered nervously.

"This is Waheed. My sister has brought great disgrace onto my family. My father is going to kill her tonight."

"No!" screamed Suleiman.

"No," he repeated in a calmer tone, looking nervously round his bedroom.

"If he does this now he could ruin everything. Can you stop him?"

"Only if I can promise him vengeance for this great dishonour."

"OK. OK. Tell him I am coming to see him tonight. I have a way he can achieve vengeance, but... but it will help stop the UK government killing more Moslems. Tell him that. If he waits, I can give him huge honour. Great dignity for your family. Can you tell him?"

"Yes. I can tell him."

"Then ask him to meet me in Brixton Mosque in one hour. OK?"

"OK. We will be there."

True to their word, all male members of the Siddiqi family were present. They gathered in the small meeting room upstairs. Suleiman had already rung ahead asking the Imam for permission to use his facilities. It was nearly time for Maghrib Prayer so they should not be disturbed.

When he entered the room, all the older men looked for somewhere to sit. Once they were comfortable Suleiman addressed them.

"I thank you for delaying what you want to do so I can speak," Suleiman began.

Ali stood to address the visitor. "Waheed said you want to stop this country killing our brothers and sisters. This is impossible."

"No," Suleiman disagreed. "No it isn't. We've almost finished our preparations. It has taken three years to organize. Both your sons are involved and they will die martyrs for Allah."

"Al-hamdulillah," echoed round the room.

"What," The Saudi asked, "Do you want to do in order to restore your family honour?"

"We, the family, must stab her to death." began an uncle. "We, the men!"

"My daughter has disgraced our fam…" Ali's voice broke.

"She must die, as is our custom." said the oldest uncle.

"We must kill her so her blood can clean away the shame." Ali said sadly.

"OK." Suleiman began, "I want to help you. I'll abduct your   daughter…"

"She has already brought enough disgrace on the family," the oldest uncle interjected.

"No." Suleiman explained, "You misunderstand me. Tariq and Waheed will come with me. We will take her to a safe place. Then you will all be brought to that place. Only the family will enter the room… but, I will film it. Then we can show the film to the world so they will learn about the justice of sharia law. Her death will be public. It will bring honour back to your family."

"You want us all to be arrested by the British police," objected the old uncle, "They do not understand our customs."

"No. Listen." The Saudi clarified, "You will all wear masks. And... and you must all prepare alibis. If you have an alibi, they can prove nothing. But I will post the video on *YouTube* to show England how sharia law works. If you do it my way, you get your vengeance... but you will also have an alibi from the 'crime'. And you help Tariq and Waheed bring sharia law to England."

"Al-ham-dulillah," echoed round the room again.

That night, Suleiman won over the doubters. The clan was sworn to secrecy on the very life-blood of Jasmine. But most important, the reputation of the whole family was about to be restored at a very high level. Honour would be satisfied. Ali smiled for the first time. Jasmine had brought dishonour on him. But he was going to purify his blood line.

30.

Saturday had been cold and wet. Sunday dawned quietly, sunny and warm, like a therapeutic bath. Mist rose from the dewy fields around the Manor. A fox tracked silently along a hedgerow adjoining Gayhurst Wood behind the mansion. It stopped. Its ears pricked up. The call for sun rise prayer echoed alien across the Home Counties countryside. Then the fox disappeared through a well-trodden gap in the foliage.

Four men met in the prayer room. They stood in a line behind the prayer mats. Then they knelt facing Mecca, while chanting incantations to Allah. After which, Imran Iqbal was welcomed to the congregation by Naveed Nazir. He showed the newcomer round the garage. Then they crossed the plaza to the stables. They inspected the completed vans very closely. Imran carefully examined the firing mechanism at the end of each firing tubes. He studied the rifling in the muzzles of each tube. The imposing figure turned and nodded to his guide. Imran could work with this delivery system. He might need to adjust the missiles to fit. But that was what he did for a living. It was what excited him. It was what challenged him. He had made innumerable explosive devices. He had killed many people in his long and illustrious career. He was on the CIA's Most Wanted list. And he had earned his reputation.

After that, Imran showed them the munitions collected the previous day. He warned them not to open the canisters. They would be exposed to dangerous levels of radiation. He further requested that he use one of the latest acquisitions, with all the seats removed for his next collection. He declared that once he had that latest delivery, he would be on the final count down. When

65

pushed, Imran said that he would only need two or three days.

That gave impetus to the crew. While they reorganised the tasks ahead, Ibrahim and Hussain got down to work. They had two vans to prepare. They stripped out all the seats and fixtures in the first van. Apart from the bench seat for the driver and his associate, everything else had to be cleared out. All projections and fixture that might scratch the load had to be removed. This was to be used to pick up Imran's latest equipment. They also secures several belts to the wall to tie equipment back. They needed to stabilise the load.

While in the second vehicle, they retained the side seats. This was to be used to transport the Siddiqi family. At the same time, they installed a bed along the middle section. It was secured to the bulkhead through the bench boltholes. This one would be used as a taxi. First, to gather the Siddiqis from different parts of the country. Second to collect Khalid and Nazir when they were due to join those in Gayhurst. Finally, it would be used to ferry Jasmine and Darren to meet their destinies.

31.

Jasmine woke to find her mother beside the bed with a cup of herbal tea.
"Come, my child. You have been crying long enough."
"But Mother, I don't love this man in Pakistan."

"How do you know? He might be the love of your life."

"It is not like your times. You were married to Dad because your father told you to…"

"Do not be disrespectful about my father. He was a good man."

"I know he was Mama. But things are different now."

"Your father and I have been happy."

"Because you know no better."

"It is the lot of women all round the world…"

"But it does not have to be. Now we want more. We want happiness and love and joy and…"

"You are dreamers. Drink up."

Jasmine took a sip. It tasted very sweet.

"You did what your father told you because you had no choice. I have a choice. I can get an education and be a doctor. I can be a teacher. I can be anything I want…"

"Of course you can my dearest. Finish your drink. But who will look after you when you are old? Ah? You must make children for the future."

"Children will come when they are ready… and not to look after me but rather for themselves."

"Yes… drink up. Why do so many of these Western marriages, these great love-love marriages end in divorce? Can you tell me?"

"That's something else… maybe… you cannot get along… I feel strange. I feel sleepy."

"It's OK my baby. Just go to sleep and soon all your problems will all be over."

32.

Naveed and Ibrahim met Waheed at the Brixton Mosque. They plotted their next move in the privacy of the small meeting room. It was imperative that nothing be said to give any clue to the British Secret Service that something was about to happen. Secrecy was the element of surprise. They needed surprise on their side for this to work.

They also discussed what would happen once they cut Tariq's tag. They assumed that an alarm would go off in the police station. That would give them little time to complete their many tasks. So they decided that it would be the last thing they do.

Half an hour later, the white windowless Ford Transit arrived outside the Siddiqi house. Ibrahim reversed it as near to the front door as possible. They trooped into the building. Tariq had already rolled his sister in a double-duvet, ready for removal. He and his brother carried her downstairs and onto the bed, in the privacy of the panel van. She was no longer their little sister. She was a traitor. A betrayer of their religion and their family.

Tariq went back to his bedroom for his bag. The journey to martyrdom was the final journey, and very few things were really necessary for such a journey. While he was composing himself, Waheed and Ibrahim carried the old couple's luggage outside. Their Ford Focus was parked in their next door neighbour's drive. Not a word was spoken. Some neighbours gathered to wave them off. The women were to be driven to their relations in Bradford. Later the men would join them. They were to establish their alibis. Then return once everything had quietened down. The Ford was driven by a female cousin. They drove off and the few spectators melted into the night.

Then Waheed went to his room to collect his bag. Suddenly, his emotions welled up. They threatened to overwhelm him. Tariq was different. He had been fighting in Syria so had already broken the umbilical cord to home. However, it was proving more difficult for Waheed. He realised that he would never come back to this home. It had been his security. This room had been his safety blanket. His family were scattered. His whole body shook with grief. Tariq entered the room and held him for a while. When the tears were dry Tariq gave him his bag and the younger brother carried their luggage downstairs.

Waheed clambered into the truck. Ibrahim returned to the house with some heavy-duty wire cutters and an electrical couplings. He knelt at Tariq's feet; first connecting the wires to the metal circuit built into the ankle tag, then he sniped through the tag and Tariq was free. They raced outside. Ibrahim leapt into the front and slammed the door. Tariq jumped into the rear of the van and pulled the double doors shut. As soon as he heard the door close, Naveed stepped on the gas.

They need not have feared. It would be over twenty-four hours before the security forces even suspected foul play.

33.

Hussain drove the bomb-maker to collect his next assignment. As before, Imran merely gave him a postcode. The driver followed the directions as they came. He did not question where they were going. From their previous experience, he knew they might be stopping anywhere. The planned rendezvous was with an arms dealer. He was ready for anything this time.

They headed south on the M1 and turned left on the London Orbital. Traffic was heavy and the going slow. They turned east at junction 29, onto the A127 Southend Arterial Road. This took them north of Basildon but they did not deviate until the Rayleigh exit on the left.

Once inside the leafy suburbs, the sat nav directed them to a huge detached house and Hussain pulled into its semi-circular front drive. They climbed out of the van and walked to the front door. From a distance it looked like a normal wood and glass front door. But closer inspection showed it was made of metal. In fact all the ground floor windows were false. They were a veneer to hide the premises of *Claremont Gun Dealership*, specialist in ex-army issue.

When the door opened, two thick set men in black suits ushered them into a modern reception area. The reception committee remained standing, their hands crossed in front of their genitalia and their backs to the door. They stared unsmiling ahead, like undertakers at a celebrity funeral.

Hussain and Imran sat on one of the settees to wait for the arms dealer to appear, which he did in dramatic style. He burst into the room, causing the newcomers to spring to their feet and the two bodyguards to rapidly reach inside their jackets. Ignoring the heightened tension he stepped forward with outstretched hand.

"Salaam Alaikum," he surprised them. He was white English with impersonal green eyes.

"Alaikum Salaam," they replied automatically.

"Imran Iqbal, I presume?"

"That's right. And you must be Allan Price."

"Correct. You asked for fifteen serviceable pistols. Unfortunately, I have not been able to get the same variety. But I managed to procure six SIG Sauer P226Rs, with six spare clips. Four Glock 17s again with four clips and five Walther PPKs with a spare clip each. There are three boxes of nine millimetre shells as requested. They are all ex-British military, decommissioned but in perfect working order; which matches your other requirement."

"Can I test fire them?"

"Of course. Reginald will take you down to the cellar. After you have fired as many of them as you want, please return here. If you are satisfied, we will hand over the weaponry and you will hand over the money. Cash only. And in used notes, as specified."

"All is as you asked," Imran replied, and Hussain hefted the black document bag for them to see. He tried to look calm, but that was not how he was feeling.

One of the bodyguards led Imran though the heavy metal doors to the hallway. After fifteen very slow minutes he returned carrying a small brown holdall. Hussain handed over the attaché case and waited while Allan counted the money. When finished he actually smiled.

"Pleasure doing business with you."

"Likewise."

Imran handed Hussain the holdall. It was heavy. They made their way into the fresh air. Once aboard the white transit, Hussain drove about a quarter of a mile on the road they had come in by. He found a pub car park where they could stop, Then tapped the next co-ordinates into the sat nav. They waited for satellite connection. While they were waiting Hussain looked in the mirror at the large open van. It meant that there was something much bigger to be collected from the next destination.

The satellite was a long time connecting…

34.

As soon as Tariq and Ibrahim slammed the rear door, Naveed pulled away. He drove past Brixton railway station. Then Naveed turned left through the one way system onto Stockwell Road. Traffic became heavier. They crossed the busy Clapham Road junction by the tube station. Then he turned left into Lansdowne Way. About half way down is a six-storey block of flats. Naveed squeezed the van onto the pavement, between two parked cars. He cut the engine.

Ibrahim beckoned to Tariq. He touched his lips in the universal sign of silence. They opened one of the rear doors and stepped down. Waheed secured the door from the inside. They wanted to conceal the duvet-roll, snoring gently in the back.
Ibrahim led the way up the concrete path into the block of flats. He opened the glass doors and Tariq moved past him. They stood at the bottom of the stairs, listening. Ibrahim leaned nearer to whisper;
"We are picking up two more guys. They must join us today."
"Fine. Who is it?"
"Khalid Ahmad. Do you know him?"
"Yes. He was in Syria with me. Well not exactly with me. We were in two separate foreign jihadi units. But I have met him."
"You get his cousin, Nazir Bashirn, into the van. I'll cut the tag off Khalid."

"OK. Are there more Mujahedeen to pick up? Only there isn't much room in the back with Jasmine on the bed."
"No. Don't worry. They can sit in the front with Naveed. Then we go straight to the manor."

Tariq nodded. They climbed two storeys to an external corridor. As they stepped along the draughty balcony, they could see out over the neighbourhood of Stockwell. Tariq looked at the untidy urban sprawl. There was nothing attractive about it. He had looked over dusty urban areas in Syria; pock-marked with bomb craters. The English were unaware of what they were doing in the Arab world. They just assumed that they had the right to impose their religion. Their politics. Their opinions. Nothing related to the culture or history of the people they dominated. Tariq wondered at the squalor of this view. What gave them the right? What gave them the assurance? The arrogance? They were unaware of what they were awakening.

Ibrahim had reached the door. They stood either side of the wooden door, but not blocking the window. Ibrahim knocked three times on the flaking brown door. Nazir opened the door wide. Then stepped aside to let them in. Ibrahim led the way down the dark corridor. It was quiet. The Ahmad family had already left for their relatives in Portsmouth. There were two bags in the hallway. Khalid stepped out of the last room. He grabbed Tariq by the shoulders and kissed him on both cheeks.

Tariq raised his eyebrows to Nazir. They picked up a case each then made for the door.

Ibrahim drew his cutters from the holdall. He knelt in front of Khalid. First, he connected the wire then snipped through the tag.

It fell away and Khalid couldn't help speaking.

"Al-ham-dulillah. Thanks be to God."

"Alhamdulillah."

The other intoned automatically then looked round guiltily. Silence was supposed to have been observed at all times. The British Secret Service could have been listening and a strange voice would alert them. Then Ibrahim led the way to the front door. They slammed it behind them and loped down the stairs after the others.

Before Naveed started the engine he produced a small holdall. Then insisted everyone put their mobile phones, battery-operated watches and all other electronic devices into it. Ibrahim passed it round. As this was being done, he extracted the batteries. He stored them in the outside pockets.

Naveed pushed the home button on the sat nav. Less than ten minutes after pulling onto the pavement in front of the flats they were bouncing down the kerb, on their way to Gayhurst Manor.

35.

According to the sat nav they were less than an hour away from their final destination. Hussain followed the instructions out of Rayleigh. They drove north, onto the A12 towards Ipswich. Then they left the dual carriageway in Colchester. They followed Westway under the railway bridge by the station. Then they followed the complex roundabout system, through a letter 'S' shape, but somehow remained on A134.

"You have now reached your destination on the left."

To Hussain's amazement, they stopped on double yellow lines on the dual carriageway. On the other side of a hedge, was a large yellow building with a white arched roof. The sign identified it as the '*Big Yellow Storage*'. It took a while to find the entrance to the storage unit. But once there, they parked near the entrance.

Several cars were dotted about the parking zone. After fifteen minutes, one of them turned on its side lights. A pale blue Mercedes-Benz drew up beside them. A heavy set man in a fawn camel hair coat and dark paisley scarf opened the rear door. He waited, looking at the van.

Imran disembarked. He walked towards the stranger. They shook hands and spoke for a short while. Imran tapped his black attaché case. The stranger nodded. He gestured towards the storage unit. They walked towards the building. Hussain hastily clambered out of the van. Two well-built men with shaven heads hurriedly left the Merc.

They made an untidy procession towards the main entrance. The man in the camel coat typed a number into the key-pad. Five men entered the yellow building. They walked in single file between numbered doorways. About halfway down on the right-hand side they stopped. The leader tapped out another number. The door clicked open. They filed into the small storeroom.

It was like a scene from *The Ipcress File*, a classic Michael Cane espionage film. There was a small wooden table and two chairs in the middle of the brightly lit space. To one side was a flatbed trolley, popular at DIY stores, and to the other a stack of long thin grey packages. They were about one and a half metres long and seven centimetres across.

"Would you like to see one?" He had an Eastern European accent.
"Yes." Imran stood holding the attaché case across his chest.
"Tomaz?" One of the bodyguards moved towards the pile then looked at Imran.
"That one." The Syrian pointed. The Albanian slid three packages to one side. He produced a knife and slit open the one indicated. Once the end was open, they carefully extricated a long tube of metal. There lay a thin, silver Lightweight Multirole Missile. Its fins were intact but its nose blunt. There was no payload attached. It lacked its warhead. Imran gave Hussain the black case and bent down to examine the rocket.

"It weighs 13 kg." The leader began his sales spiel. "It is 1.3m long by 0.076m diameter. And it is capable of delivering a three kilogram warhead. It is the most popular lightweight missile in NATO. Thoroughly dependable. You ordered twenty-eight. What do you think?"

"It is as we required. Here is the money. Please check it."

"Oh! I will. Don't worry."

The man in the camel-haired coat sat at the table. Then beckoned Imran to sit opposite him. The case was opened. The arms dealer began to count a random batch. Then he counted another bundle from the bottom of the case. Then he stacked the batches in front of him. Lastly he counted them into his own sports bag.

"Fine. Tomaz, help them load up."

The Albanians began stacking the packages on their flatbed trolley. They were not heavy, just awkward to handle.

Hussain wandered back to the van. He reversed it to the entrance door. Then jumped out of the cab. He ran round to the rear to fling both doors wide open.

The two body guards wheeled the flatbed out of the main doors. They pushed it up to the open doors of the white van. Hussain helped them load the twenty-eight oblong packages aboard. He secured the rear of the van as they returned to the unit.

Hussain climbed back into the driver's seat. He turned the ignition key to activate the electrics, but not start the motor. Then he tapped the co-ordinates for Gayhurst into the sat nav.

Pretty soon he watched Imran leave the building in his wing mirror. The bomb maker climbed aboard in beside him. He nodded so the driver turned the engine on.

They made their way towards the A12 for the homeward journey.

36.

After that wet windy morning, the afternoon was turning out to be quite pleasant. The journey to Gayhurst was uneventful. After the gates juddered open, Naveed drove through the arched entrance. He steered round the fountain, stopping outside the main entrance.

The rear door opened. Tariq stepped out. Then he helped Waheed carry the stretcher into the watery sunshine. Jasmine was just beginning to stir. The drugs were wearing off. Ibrahim led them to the left hand side of the grand main entrance sandstone stairway. They entered a smaller door. It was the ground floor service entrance. The Siddiqi brothers carried their sister into the bowels of the Manor House.

Meanwhile, Khalid and Nazir climbed out of the front, off-side door. Both stretched the stiffness out of their joints.

It had been a cramped journey. They gazed round at their new home. Then watched the Siddiqi brothers disappear down-stairs. They retrieved their bags from the van. Then carried them into the reception area. Naveed led them through to the kitchen. He put the kettle on. Then took some savoury snacks from the fridge. He asked the newcomers to help themselves to refreshments as the cook was needed elsewhere.

Ibrahim left the latest recruits in the kitchen. He took the back stairs to the cellar and then opened the door in the spacious front cellar. It was lined with red brick, containing many niches and alcoves. For many years it had housed a fine collection of rare wines. Now it was empty. The air was dry but musty. There was a metal framed bedstead. On it was a thin mattress and a blanket on the bed. Next to it was a commode chair. While above the bed was a large metal ring embedded into the solid stone wall. From this a thick chain hung down the wall like a sleeping python.

The Siddiqis had already placed their sister on the bed. Waheed covered her with the blanket. Tariq secured a heavy-duty manacle at the end of the chain round her left wrist. She moaned and her breathing had become more laboured.

Ibrahim prepared a syringe. Once the brothers stepped aside he injected *Flunitrazepam* into a vein on her left wrist. Gradually her breathing became more regular.

Naveed walked in to survey their work. He nodded. Everyone left Jasmine to her slumbers.

Upon returning upstairs, Ibrahim took charge in the kitchen. He used the boiling water from the kettle to half fill a pan. This was put on the stove to re-boil. He took a packet of rice from the cupboard. This was placed near the heating pan. Then he got some chicken breasts out of the fridge. They had been marinating in a brown sauce. Ibrahim placed them under the grill.

The four guests carried their bags up to the first floor. Naveed showed Tariq and Waheed to the third door on the left, while Khalid and Nazir were billeted directly across the corridor. They were shown the communal bathroom. He told them to make their way downstairs as soon as they had freshened up.

37.

Fifteen minutes later, Hussain pulled in behind the first van. He led Imran up the main steps and into the imposing entrance. They walked single file into the communal sitting room where everyone was congregating.

Naveed made the introductions. All the fighters had heard of Imran so were intrigued he was involved with the plan. They gathered round to question him and to hear his anecdotes of the Syrian War.

Now everyone was there, Ibrahim went to the kitchen to finalise preparations. Hussain called for volunteers to off-load the weapons. They followed Imran out to unload the cargo. Hussain went into the kitchen to set the dining room for eight.

As experienced soldiers, Tariq and Khalid were interested to see what they would be using. They had both used hand-held rocket launchers so were familiar with missiles. But although these were light-weight projectiles, they were longer and more powerful than the Islamic State had in Syria.

Imran also showed them the pistols. He explained that he wanted them all familiar with the armaments within the next few days. They divided themselves into pairs to carry the long packages from the van and into the arsenal in the basement.

The cellar was divided in two. The bigger room had been the main wine cellar when the manor was first designed and because it was dry and cool it was ideal for storing weapons. They moved all the wooden wine racks to the rear wall. This opened up the space. Imran commandeered a long trestle table. He planned to manufacture explosive devices. But in the meantime, he directed the missiles be laid to the right of the table. Then they stacked the warheads on the left.

Against the wall, just inside the door, were the launch tubes. They were stacked in groups of four. Each group would be fitted to every assault vehicle. There were only four sets left. So the pile would get smaller. That meant

Imran could expand his store, if it were needed. He seemed pleased with the facilities.

The smaller front cellar was more secure so they were using that as a prison for Jasmine. They were also using it as a store for unwanted bulky fittings from the van conversions. But because she was there, they were to be temporarily stacked in the corridor outside.

38.

Faisal Khan disliked Mondays in general, but this morning in particular. Drizzle had turned to a soaking shower as he cycled through Lambeth. He arrived at Thames House wet through. But, once he showered and towelled vigorously he felt ready for the day. He took the stairs two at a time right up to the third floor. This morning the Forsyth twins were in their female personas.
"Good morning ladies. Dismal day." Faisal gazed into the eye scanner, waiting for the security door to open.
"Good morning Mr Khan," Michael replied, his voice light and airy.
"Yes it is," added Francis wistfully.

The door slid open and Faisal stepped into the antechamber. He turned as the semi-circular door swished round him. Then stepped through into his department. Before getting a coffee, he switched on his equipment. He liked to give it time to warm up. It always took time to connect through all the security systems. When it had settled itself he could access the extranet.

Very soon he was listening into the recordings of his Syrians. It was longer than usual because of the weekend. At the same time he was fast forwarding though the videos of those detainees who warranted closer scrutiny. It was not long before he realised something was seriously wrong at the Siddiqi household. It became apparent that Tarik had vanished from his room the previous morning.

"Shit. Shit. Shit." To himself, then much louder, "Ma'am?"
Faisal called the last word across the open planned office. His colleagues stopped what they were doing to stare at him. Jo Pullen emerged from her office and threaded her way between desks.

"What's the matter with you Faisal? You know better than shout across..." she began to admonish him.
"Tarik's gone."
"What? Let me see."
She pulled a wheelie chair to Faisal's station. He replayed the second half of the weekend in Tarik's room. They watched as Tarik quickly packed a bag. Waheed collected it. Then he left the bedroom. Faisal then fast forwarded the recording to show that he had not returned.

"OK. Go through all the audio recordings, perhaps we can learn something from them." She pushed herself up and addressed the room. "It looks like one of our tagged Syrian veterans has done a runner. Check the rest. Let's hope he is the only one. Malcolm?" she called to another intelligence officer at the coffee machine. "Sign out a car. I'll meet you outside in five minutes."

39.

Naveed led Tariq and Waheed out to the workshop. He took them to the left-hand work bench. He told them to collect the van roof. It was placed across the wooden worktop. Next they were instructed to collect four launch tubes from the armament store. They disappeared out of the workroom and collected the tubes from Imran's workshop. He was busy and only grunted in response to their greetings. It took them two journeys to get all four metal pipes.

Using a template Naveed marked out the points to attach the fittings. He got the brothers to repeat the process three more times across the roof top. Then he produced three visors that could be clipped to their helmets. Once their eyes were protected, he lit the oxy-acetylene torch and prepared to weld the first of the eight fittings to the roof. The intense white light lit up their masked faces, making them look like something from a Soviet Union documentary about working class heroes of industry. They fixed the first metal clamp in place.

Then he stepped back and handed the torch to Tariq. He watched as they did the second one. Once satisfied that they knew what they were doing, he went to the right-hand work station to continue adapting fittings for the next roof fixtures.

While they were doing that, Ibrahim had taken Khalid and Nazir to the garage, on the other side of the quad. He clicked on the fluorescent lights to reveal five completed vehicles, their tubes welded to their roofs. However, two were scarred with the welding sites. Two more had material taped over their light fittings and windows. Ibrahim kitted them out with paint splattered blue overalls and nose masks. Then he showed them the paint-spray guns. They loaded two with white paint. By moving the gun from side to side, Ibrahim demonstrated how to apply an even cover of paint without over-painting and causing runs. As soon as they understood, the supervisor went over to the vehicle that had already been done. He made sure the paint was completely dry then carefully removed all the protective tape in preparation for the next stage in the process.

40.

Like most Intelligence and Mobile Surveillance Officers working for MI5, Malcolm Brainchild had taken the advanced driver's course. He easily negotiated the backstreets of Brixton at speed. They screeched to a halt outside Tariq's home. The curtains were drawn.

Jo knocked loudly on the front door. When there was no answer she lifted her chin to the side gate and Malcolm disappeared along the passageway to the rear of the property. She tried the door handle. It was locked. She rang the bell then squinted though the lace curtains in the downstairs windows before returning to the door again. She heard movement inside. Malcolm appeared briefly as the door yawned ajar and she slipped inside, closing it firmly behind her.

Malcolm already had his blue crime-scene gloves on. Jo wriggled her fingers into a pair of pale blue, thin rubber gloves. They systematically searched the building.

"There is no dirty washing," observed Malcolm.

"Looks like a planned exit," confirmed the project manager.

"Clothing's missing. We need to interview neighbours and workmates to find out where they might have gone," he pointed out. "We are going to need the local Bobbies in on this one."

"Yes," she agreed. "We haven't got the manpower to search all transport hubs and visit all friends and relations. Ummm. OK. Let's remove all our devices."

Malcolm went out to the dark blue Ford S-MAX Titanium to retrieve a medium sized light tan suitcase. He noticed several neighbours had begun to gather but did not mind because it would be less likely that someone would try to interfere with the car with so many witnesses.

"Beginning to collect an audience," he observed as he strode into the kitchen.

"Better make it snappy then. You do the cameras. I'll do the microphones."

He opened the case and took out two smoke detectors. Standing on one of the kitchen chairs, he unscrewed the ceiling fitting outside the kitchen and put back the one he had taken down nine months earlier. They would have to examine it to see why it stopped working six months before. Carrying the chair with him, Malcolm went into Tariq's bedroom and replaced that one too.

When he got back to the kitchen Jo was packing the fittings she had collected. He put his in the suitcase.

"OK?" Jo asked. "Good. Let's put everything back in order. Lock up and wait outside, like good law-abiding citizens, for The Old Bill to arrive."

"Wouldn't do any harm interviewing the neighbours."

"Good idea. If we look official they might forget that we have been inside."

"Umm. Maybe."

He picked up the bag and went out the back way, relocking doors as he went. She scanned round to make sure everything looked undisturbed then left by the front door, making sure it closed properly behind her.

41.

Although there is an Ecumenical Committee working for the British government, it is dominated by the Church of England hierarchy. There are Catholic, Moslem and Jewish Members but together they form a minority. There are no government committees dealing with Islam per se. Apart that is from those attached to the Home Office. They regard it purely as a security threat. They are seeking extremists within the faith. So Lord Leyton has taken it upon himself to act as a one-man committee. He aims to bring Islam into the forefront of British life, where he considers it belongs. The connotation of a 'British Moslem' should be positive. Yet whenever those two words are connected in the British media, it is negative

Suleiman was driving His Lordship to the Finsbury Park Mosque for a meeting with the Imams. The peer was interested in their attempts to deal with their tarnished reputation. Even today, when Finsbury Park is mentioned, Abu Hamza al-Masri springs to mind. That one-armed preacher epitomized all that was wrong with the religion. Yet he was Imam during the 1990s. No matter what they do, his negative legacy lingers on.

Lord Kabir Anwar specifically wanted to see what they were doing about the radicalisation of young Moslems in the area. When the chauffeur was informed about the trip the previous evening he had phoned round to set up one of his impromptu meetings. By arranging rendezvous when the peer toured Britain, he concealed his activities from the authorities. He used Kabir Anwar as a smoke screen to meet with his army of collaborators.

They pulled into the driveway to the right of the mosque. The wrought iron gates shut behind them. The chauffeur opened the rear door and Kabir stepped into the arms of Mohammed, the present Imam. They embraced, then the nobleman was introduced to the Elders of the Mosque. They went in together. Suleiman followed them upstairs. He allowed himself to drop to the back of the group. Then slipped into one of the meeting rooms where five men were waiting for him.

"As-salam-o-alaikum," he greeted them.

"Alaykumu salam," they replied, coming forward to shake his hand or kiss his cheek, depending on their birth culture.

He apologised for calling the meeting with such short notice. Then added that he was short of time. He explained that The Plan had been brought forward because all personnel were now in place. Now they were working on the project, a more realistic timetable could be followed. Smiles began to radiate round the room. It was as though the sun had emerged from behind a cloud. They

90

had been frustrated by the apparent inactivity. Now, at last, there was action.

Suleiman outlined his plan to pick them up within the week. He told them to prepare their respective warriors. They were liaising with two more Syrian veterans, tagged in their respective homes. He clarified that they would be picked up too. But the Saudi reminded them about saying too much because the British Secret Service had bugged their homes.

He informed them that the code word for anyone contacting them on his behalf would be 'Al-Hilal'. This, he reminded them, is Arabic for 'Crescent Moon'. That is the emblem to be found on top of every mosque in the world. It is the enduring symbol of Islam. So he had adopted it as the name of his attack on England.

"Alhamdulillah," They rejoiced, "Allah be praised," echoed round the room.

42.

When Jo and Malcolm return to Thames House, Faisal Khan greeted them with a beckoning finger.
"I've found something. Might explain the mass exit."
The unit boss dragged over a wheelie chair to listen to a muffled conversation in the Siddiqi living room.

"That microphone is playing up. We must examine it..." Malcolm observed.

"Shh! Listen," Faisal interjected.

They could hear the emotion in Jasmine's voice as she reasoned with her father.

"So. An arranged marriage," observed Jo. "Is this what it's about?"

"I think we are missing something," pondered Malcolm.

"Hey!" called David from the adjacent work station, "This might be your missing link."

And he turned up the speakers. A hissing sound breathed ominously through the office.

"Nothing? What did you want to tell us?" asked Jo.

"Khalid Ahmad has also disappeared."

"When?" asked Faisal.

"Sunday afternoon."

"Same time. This isn't an arranged marriage. Something is going down. We need to find where our boys have gone.

"OK Everyone," Jo called across the open plan office. "Recheck all our Syrians to see if any more disappeared yesterday. Then use all your contacts to see if we can trace Tariq Siddiqi and Khalid Ahmad. Where did their families go?"

"He was living with his cousin Nazir Bashirn," David explained, "Who has not been to Syria. That is why the authorities allowed them to share."

"Has Nazir gone too?"

"Can't tell. The house has been totally silent since Sunday afternoon."

"What's your best guess?"

"I can't see them separating. Look, it's never been this quiet. Also… also Nazir's family seem to have gone too."

"OK. Malcolm. Get the car again. I'll meet you out front. We need to check Khalid's place before we inform the Metropolitan Police. And the rest of you… if you find another absconder… let us know immediately. Then we can act before coming back here. OK? Let's go."

Her high heels clicked out an aggressive staccato tattoo as every eye watched her retrace her steps through the entrance vestibule.

43.

The Shah brothers wandered out of the mosque after Suleiman joined the entourage. They turned left and followed St Thomas's Road to the traffic lights then right onto Seven Sisters Road.

"What was it like in Syria?" Sahid asked his older brother.

"I told you before," Shami looked over his shoulder, "Don't mention it."

He had entered UK directly from Saudi Arabia. It meant that the British authorities had not connected him to the IS war.

"I don't want anyone to know I have been there."

"I know bro', but we can't be overheard here."

"Well." He relaxed a little, "War is never easy. It was tough at times. Hand to hand fighting with fierce troops. But it made me determined that we have to bring the war here."

"Are you excited by what Suleiman said?"

"Alhamdulillah. It is the answer to all my prayers. And I know many veterans feel the same. What about you?"

"Alhamdulillah. It is great."

"Do you want to be a martyr?"

"Of course. Why do you question me?"

Shami noticed that Sahid had seemed agitated for a while.

"You can still be a good Moslem and not want to be a martyr."

"You fought for Islam against the Infidel. I want to. Remember I was going to join you but the British authorities asked too many questions. So I could not come."

"I remember."

"So I wanted to be a martyr."

" I do not question that. But their may be another time...another cause that you think is better for martyrdom."

"Look, I have to see someone," The younger brother said, "OK? See you later."

Sahid turned into Queen's Drive and strode alongside the five-storey block of flats with their distinctive green balconies. Shami continued until he was out of sight but stopped in his tracks. Something about his brother's

94

behaviour niggled in the back of his mind. He had asked about the war, a taboo subject between them. Then he had gone off before the conversation really got started. But it was his eyes.

Shami's senses had been heightened by his war experiences. Sometimes it was as though everything was in slow motion. At other times he could see a face in the crowd clearly. But now he knew he had to follow his brother. Sahid was hiding something. There was something he was not sharing with his older brother.

Shami turned on his heel and came level with the end of the flats, just in time to see his brother striding through the gates half way along the block. He jog trotted as far as the second to last brick column. It was just before the gatepost, in the perimeter railings. He stopped to look. His brother was already half-way along. Then he stopped and turned. Shami ducked back and counted to three. He peeped again. Sahid was talking into an intercom speaker beside the doors. Then pulled open the door and went inside.

Shami broke cover and ran to the door. He saw the lift inside. A number three glowed through the reinforced glass. He pushed all the apartment buttons. Hoping someone would respond... and they did. The door clicked. He pulled it open and stepped inside.

By the time he sprinted up to the third floor, he was out of breath. He regretted not keeping so fit. All the time he had been abroad he had been in super condition. Now he was getting slower. That was another reason to take on this mission. Before he lost all his sharpness.

Shami tugged open the glass door and peered round. Nothing. He tiptoed along the gallery ducking past windows. Until he came close to the last door on the right. Music pulsated through the very walls.

He stopped and waited. Then he could smell cannabis. He did not need to find out more. Shami carefully retraced his steps. He put as much distance between himself and the flats as possible. He might have felt that he was getting unhealthy waiting for something to happen. But now he felt that cold anger. That calculating emotion, where he could remain aloof of the reality. To a certain extent, all soldiers know this detachment. Otherwise how could they justify killing another human being. It is especially strong with those soldiers who have been involved with hand to hand combat. You cannot smell your enemy. You cannot look into his eyes. You cannot feel his breath on your cheek. You are never the same again.

The only thing Shami was sure about was that the people in that flat were going to die. He just had not decided whether to involve Suleiman or do it himself.

44.

Naveed inspected the finished roof.

"You should have done this professionally." He smiled at the brothers, "OK. We need to get the infidel who ruined your sister. But you have to shave off your beards first."

"Wallah!" exclaimed Tariq. "I am a good Moslem and I would never…"

"In that case you can't pick up the infidel."

"You have a beard."

"This is designer stubble, not a beard. I shaved my full beard off when I came to UK." Naveed wanted them to blend in, "Also I am not known to the Secret Service. At least, not in this country. It's up to you. If you want to pick him up, shave off your beard. Then meet me outside. I will wait for one hour. If you do not show, I will do it myself."

Half an hour later Tariq and Waheed climbed into the back of the van. They looked much younger without their untidy beards. Both men kept touching their faces. They commented on how cold it was.

Waheed recognised the van as the same one they had used to abduct Jasmine. Naveed had replaced the stretcher on the bed. It would more than suffice to transport Darren in the same way. The co-ordinates for Brixton station were tapped into the sat nav. That would be near enough to capture Darren. As soon as the GPS system for navigation activated, he drove through the arch on their way to London.

Darren was surprised when Waheed walked into his bedroom.

"What are you doing here?"

"Do you know me?" Waheed asked.

"Yes of course. You used to go to my school. You are Jasmine's big brother."

"Yeh. Well… she sent me…"

"What's the matter? Where is she? I haven't seen her for two days. She always pops in here. Every day."

"Well she needs to see you."

"I need to see that she is alright. Where is she?"

"Not far. But we have to hurry."

"Where is…"

"There's no time to explain. Come on."

Darren still hesitated. Waheed paused at the door.

"This is your last chance to see her before she goes to Pakistan."

Then turned and went downstairs. Darren lunged for his jacket and followed Jasmine's brother.

There was a plain white van parked outside the back gate. Waheed half opened the rear door. Darren moved to get in and Waheed suddenly pushed him. Tariq threw him to the floor and sat on him. Hussain thrust a hypodermic of *Flunitrazepam* into his arm. Waheed scrambled into the open space and slammed the door shut. Darren started screaming so Tariq sat on his face and Waheed sat on his legs. Slowly his thrashing subsided.

Hussain squeezed himself into the driver's seat. The satellite navigation system was already programmed. The map glowed. Tariq and Waheed rolled the inert body into a duvet. Then they struggled to lift him like a roll of carpet. But unlike a roll of carpet he was a dead weight and sagged in the middle. The van lurched forward and they dropped him. Praying out loud Tariq grabbed the inert package and thrust it at the bed. Waheed flung the feet after it. The bundle lay on the bed. The brothers sat back on either side, breathing heavily.

45.

Faisal and David returned to the office after lunch.
"Well?" Jo asked as she strode towards them.
"Just returned from the school," David began. "Jasmine wasn't there today."
"OK. Anything else?"
"Yep."
"Well?" She waited… then said. "Hell's Bells Faisal. It's like extracting hen's teeth."
"I've identified Darren."
"Darren?"
"Yes. Jasmine's boyfriend."
"Darren," Jo repeated, "An unbeliever. No wonder the family's in such a tizwaz."
"It may account for the arranged marriage," David volunteered.

"Could be."

"One of Jasmine's friends told us about Darren," Faisal elaborated, "I had heard something on the recording, but it was too indistinct. As soon as she said the name, it clicked."

"Good." Jo decided, "As you guys identified him, go and have a chat to him. If we can find her, we might be able to locate Tariq."

46.

After lunch at the mosque, Lord Anwar wanted to return to Westminster. As a member of the Energy and Climate Change Committee it was imperative that he attend the debate about the proliferation of 'small' nuclear power stations. As he disembarked from the luxury of the Bentley he dismissed his driver for the rest of the day.

Suleiman did not leave the parking bay immediately. He took out his emergency phone. There was a text message from Shami. He read it with growing alarm. Why were things becoming so complicated, he wondered. He answered the text. He told Shami to meet him at the entrance to Finsbury Park. The one that was nearest the mosque, in an hour.

Forty-five minutes later, he was driving under the railway bridge. Then followed the Seven Sisters to Manor House Tube station. Here he turned left onto Green Lane. Next, left again on Endymion Road. Finally, he parked near the

London Blitz American Football Club. It was just a short distance to the gates. He could see Shami waiting just inside the gates facing the road. It looked like he was hiding.

"Salaam Shami."

"Salaam Suleiman."

They touched right cheeks as was the Saudi custom.

"What is the problem?"

"Let us walk." Sami led him back into the park. "I followed my brother to a drugs den."

"Is he taking drugs?"

"I think so. Yes. He has become moody since we agreed to join you."

"Is he going to pray? He mustn't go to prayer in the mosque if he is taking drugs. Anyone going to pray, must be clean."

"Yes he is going to every prayer call at the mosque with me. Five times a day!"

"You must stop him."

"I want to kill all the drug dealers. They are poisoning young Moslems. That is why I went to Syria."

"To kill drug dealers?"

"No. I wanted to learn to kill. Then I wanted to clean up the streets of London."

"Allah the gracious will look kindly on your good heart."

"What shall I do?"

"Stop Sahid going to the mosque. Try to free him from drugs. We need him healthy for our mission."

"And the dealers?"

"I haven't decided... but that might be another good lesson to teach the British people. We need to show them the strengths of sharia law. This could be Allah sent. Leave it with me."

"Thank you Suleiman."

"Stay in the peace of Allah."

"Salaam."

They shook hands and went their separate ways. Suleiman looked preoccupied as he returned to the Bentley.

47.

Naveed finished preparing the firing tubes ready for the last two vans. The alarm on his watch bleeped twice. He looked at the time. Then called the others for prayer. But first they traipsed down to the ablution room, adjacent to the kitchen. They washed their hands and feet. They rubbed water across their eyes, noses, mouths and ears preparing themselves to pray. As the senior Imam, Imran led the prayer.

Naveed asked Ibrahim to prepare some simple food and a drink for Jasmine. The cook heated up some rice and chicken and poured out a tin-mug full of sweetened tea. He arranged them on a tray.

Naveed escorted Ibrahim down to the cellar. As they entered, Naveed turned on the light. Jasmine made a noise. At least she was awake.

"I want to go to the toilet," she whined as her hand shielded her eyes against the unaccustomed glare.

"Use the commode beside the bed," Naveed said.

She squinted sideways at it.

"I can't go in that dirty thing."

"Then soil yourself. I don't care. Here is your food."

"I don't like tea."

"Then you will die of dehydration. It's up to you."

And the two men left. Then they returned thirty minutes later. The food and drink had gone. Ibrahim stood with the tray. Naveed took a hypodermic from his case. He drew some *Flunitrazepam* from a small phial. He tapped the barrel.

"No. Don't drug me again," she begged, "I can't think straight. Are you going to hurt me? Don't hurt me. Please. No...."

She slumped sideways and Naveed pulled her body straight on the bed. He took the bucket from under the commode seat emptied it into the wall sink, washed it out then replaced it in the furniture. Ibrahim flushed the material down the sink then poured disinfectant down the drain.

The men left to the gentle snoring of the drugged girl, and switched out the light.

48.

Faisal sat on Darren's bed scanning round the room to see if there was anything he had missed. The boy's parents had confirmed that his bomber jacket was missing. They also confirmed that it was very unusual for him to go out for so long without telling them.

Faisal had a horrible feeling about this. But first things first. He needed the parent's co-operation. They were honest hard-working folk. So he did not want to unduly alarm them. The only thing to do was leave his calling card. He ask them to phone him when their son showed up. It was possible that he had popped out to the shops. But deep down Faisal knew differently. He had observed Darren's phone was still on charge. And his tablet lay on the table. He was absolutely sure that being a modern youngster, he would have at least taken one with him. And as he had left them, the Security Services could not track him. That was a great disappointment. He had hoped to discover his phone number. An hour had passed since they had come and they were no nearer Darren.

The vibrations from his own phone began to shudder urgently in his left pocket. He pulled it out. One letter shimmied on the screen. It was one of his informants. He could not let this pass. He pressed the handset symbol and waited.

He wondered why they used an old fashioned technology symbol for this new telephone. Then it was answered.

"Ali Baba?" Faisal asked.
"Wicked Uncle?" the disembodied voice echoed distorted, "We had a meeting today. I think you will like to know."
"Can you tell me who was at the meeting?"
"No time. Same place. Eight tonight."
"OK. I'll be there."
And the phone went dead.

Faisal slipped it back into his pocket. Stood and looked round the room again. There was nothing that gave him any idea where Darren had gone. Shaking his head with frustration, he wandered down to the café.

49.

Hussain pulled up behind the other white van. Tariq and Waheed had strapped the duvet roll to the stretcher. It was easier to handle because it was rigid. They carried out of the van and though the tradesman's entrance. Hussain led the way down to the detention cellar. He opened doors for the brothers. They manoeuvred their load into the dark depths of the building.

By the time they arrived, Naveed had already unlocked the cellar door. He held it open for them. He indicated a bunk bed on the other side of the room from Jasmine. They placed the stretcher beside the bed. Tariq pulled the duvet upwards. Darren spun round, until he tumbled out onto the cold flag-stones. They picked him up and placed him on the mattress.

As with the other bed, there was a commode to one side, and a chain attached to a large iron ring set into the wall above. Once manacled to the bedstead he would be able to stand up and get to the toilet, but not much else.

Naveed listened to his breathing. He pinched the skin of the eye lid. Darren moved his head and made one or two whimpering noises.

Naveed took out a hypodermic syringe and administered another dose of *Flunitrazepam*. He felt it would be enough to keep him incapacitated until the morning.

Then he went across to feel Jasmine's pulse before beckoning everyone to leave the cellar. One last look around and he switched off the fluorescent lights, plunging the basement into impenetrable blackness.

In the silence of the dark, two lovers breathed deeply, unaware of each other.

50.

Josephine Pullen ran her fingers through her hair. It looked like two of her tagged Syrians had been sprung. On top of this, the whole Siddiqi family and Nazir's parents had disappeared off the face of the earth. She did not have the manpower to follow all the leads that were left dangling. She also felt very vulnerable, a relative newcomer to MI5, taking on this highly sensitive department. Not for the first time she wondered if she had been put there as a scapegoat should anything go wrong.

"Excuse me ma'am." Tom Canning was standing in front of her desk.

"Yes Tom. What can I do for you?"

"Roger Banter, from Computer Intelligence says they can't crack the code."

"Can't?"

"Apparently it is new and they cannot crack it with the present software."

"So?" She turned her palms upwards in a gesture of incomprehension.

"Well." He tried. "I know someone from GCHQ who might be able to help. But it might take a bit of time."

"You know, I can't believe this Tom. Here we are, working for one of the most sophisticated Security Services in the whole world and Computer Intelligence merely send the recoding back to say they don't know what it is... Unbelievable."

"I'll e-mail my friend this evening to see if she can help. OK?"

"Thanks Tom. I'm not getting at you but you would have thought that in this day and age that we could have risen above the old boy network."

"Sorry?"

"Well, we have to rely on you knowing somebody. What would have happened if you didn't work here? What then?"

Tom pulled a face. She smiled and continued.

"OK Tom you win. Old boy's network it is. Let me know what your friend says."

"There's one small problem…"

"Which is?"

"I'll have to take the memory stick out of the office…"

"For God's sake don't leave it on a train or we will never hear the last of it."

"Thank you ma'am."

She nodded and Tom left the office firmly putting the memory stick deep into his right-hand trouser pocket. She blinked, then smiled. The little rascal she thought. He has already copied it onto a memory stick.

51.

Suleiman dialled a familiar number.

"Naveed?"

"We have just welcomed our new guest."

"Good. How is he?" Suleiman wanted to know.

"Ready for tomorrow," Was the careful answer.

"Good. There has been a development. We have to bring things forward by a week. We will collect the second batch tomorrow."

"That's good. They can help with the conversions. But I'm not sure we can have everything ready that quickly."

"I didn't mean the whole plan. Just the pick-ups."

"OK. But British Security will have longer to search for them."

"Can't be helped. It is more important to make sure we have the full complement. We need the numbers... and the experience. And get them all shaved. That will delay identification."

"OK," agreed Naveed, "We will pick them up tomorrow morning."

"Make sure you have enough weapons for everyone... and make sure you bring some sharp Jambiyas."

"Are we going to kill some meat?"

"We are going to kill some men."

"Do you want me to bring the camera?" Naveed wanted to know.

"That is the most important part."

"I understand."

"Tomorrow, in Finsbury Park," Suleiman confirmed.

"As-salam-o-alaikum."

"Alaykumu salam," Suleiman answered automatically. He disconnected. Slid open the phone and extracted the SIM card. It went into his left-hand pocket, ready to shred later.

52.

By a strange twist of fate, Faisal parked his car in almost the same place as Suleiman had two hours before. He walked out of the park and turned right. He entered the *'Twelve Pins'*, an old fashioned Victorian pub near Finsbury Park tube station.

The reason they had chosen this rendezvous was that no self-respecting Moslem would be seen dead in a pub like this. Faisal ordered a pint of *Bombardier* and a black coffee for his informant. It was quite busy and it took a while for him to be served.

Finally, he took the drinks to a table as far from the door as possible. Although no Moslem would enter this den of iniquity, they might pass the front door and look in. They must not be seen together.

Then the intelligence officer sat back and relaxed for the first time that day. He sipped the real ale appreciatively, pondering the quick turn of events, especially discovering Darren. Only later, when he knew the name did he hear it clearly on the tape. It just showed how easy it is to miss vital information when you think you are concentrating.

"Hello Mr. Khan." His informant looked sheepish.

"Welcome. Sit down. I've got you a coffee."

"I can't stay long. I only popped out for some cigarettes."

"OK. What have you got?"

"The Saudi called a meeting today in Finsbury Park Mosque."

"How many attended?"

"About five."

"About?"

"Five. Yes. We are going to move soon."

"Who is this Saudi?"

"I don't know. He has a big car, so he is very rich."

"Number plate?"

"I don't know. He said that we will be contacted by someone else. And he will say 'Hilal'."

"Hilal?"

"Yes. 'Crescent Moon'. The symbol of Islam."

"I know what 'Hilal' means. Why would he need passwords?"

"I must go now," and he started to rise.

"Here," Faisal rummaged in his pocket and took out a jeweller's box. "Take this wrist watch. If you are suddenly whisked away, turn it on... by winding this button backwards. Remember, wind it backwards. Then I will easily find you. OK? I will keep you safe."

"Thank you Mr Khan."

"And here is twenty quid for your efforts tonight."

"Thank you Mr. Khan."

And with that, his informant disappeared through the crowd towards the door. Faisal took another swig of his drink. He noticed that the coffee was untouched, so drank that too.

Waste not, want not, as his grandpa used to say.

53.

On the stroke of six on that misty Tuesday morning, Hussain and Tarik boarded the Land Cruiser. They drove it through the clock-tower archway and turned left. Naveed closed the gates behind them. He slotted home the heavy-duty wooden bar then wandered inside the workshop. They were not expecting any guests today. He was directing all the new manpower into finishing the vans as soon as possible.

Tarik glanced at the sat nav. They were due to arrive at ten to nine. He waited until Hussain was heading north on the M1 before he took out the mobile phone. Naveed included explicit instructions on handing it to him. Tarik dialled his uncle's number. As soon as he heard the familiar voice he told him to listen. The instructions were simple. Gather all their male relatives at his house at nine. Then hung up. He removed the SIM card and tossed it out of the window.

They made one stop at the Tibshelf Service Station. The driver had been complaining about feeling tired. He felt that a break and some caffeine would help wake him up. They ordered a black tea for Hussain and still water for Tariq. They also took the opportunity to use the toilet. Since his years fighting in the Syrian desert, Tariq had a bladder problem. There had been times when he had to refrain from urinating. The smell might attract unwanted attention. Or a damp patch on the sand. Whatever the cause, he now had to use the toilet every two hours. Often waking up three or four times at night.

However, they were soon on the road again. Despite the rush hour traffic, they arrived at fifteen minutes past nine.

Tariq embraced the sombre gathering of elders from his extended family. They discussed who should go with Ali Siddiqi to punish his daughter's transgressions. In the end, eight members of the family, one from each branch, would witness his vengeance.

Those remaining were to provide alibis for the avengers. Likewise, all families were to be seen frequently every day, out and about. But they were to remain silent about what was about to happen.

Anyone informing the authorities or gossiping to neighbours about it were condemning themselves to the same fate. Even when the video became public, the family secret had to remain just that. The older generations were sworn to secrecy on the lives of their children. It was the most revered vow a man can make in Pakistani Moslem tradition. It meant that he might be executed for any lapse; but so too all his male heirs. No one was going to break that vow.

54.

Imran took Khalid and Nazir into the cellar. Over the last twenty-four hours, he had rearranged it. There was his armament's workshop and munitions store. In the latter were piles of bunker-busting warheads, tubes to fix on the van roofs, stacks of Lightweight Multirole Missiles, a case containing various pistols and 9mm ammunition.

However, along the back wall he had set up a shooting gallery. The target was a dilapidated shop's dummy propped up against a stack of sandbags.

He showed the Mujahedeen the SIG Sauer P226R pistols he had been cleaning. Each gun could shoot fifteen rounds. He also gave them one spare ammunition clip each. Although Khalid had used many different firearms in Syria, this was the first time he had the opportunity to use a handgun. He hefted it up and down to become familiar with the weight.

Nazir, on the other hand, had never fired a gun in his life. Imran showed him how to stand, squarely facing the dummy. He held the butt in his right hand and the left hand cupped underneath. It was to reduce any shaking. Then he gave him some yellow fluffy earmuffs. He showed Nazir how to squeeze the trigger, not 'pull' it. The blasts of the gun were deafening in the confines of the cellar. The young want-to-be fighter flinched under the shear physicality of the sound. But he was hitting the dummy's abdominal area by the end of the first magazine.

Imran's advice had been to shoot at the belt buckle and you are sure to hit something solid.

Then he asked Khalid to fire. As an experienced urban fighter he was not fazed by the request. He stood sideways on then lifted his right arm. Then fired off three shots in rapid succession without flinching. Three lumps of plastic disintegrated from the chest area of the dummy. The armourer declared himself satisfied. He gave each of them a handful of shells and showed them how to fill the magazines.

They were then fitted out with a shoulder holster each. Imran then spent some time adjusting the straps. He pointed out that they would have to leave the van so did not want to alarm the general public. Also, with a concealed weapon, they would have the element of surprise, should an emergency arise.

Imran's final instruction was to wear the gun at all times. He maintained that it would eventually become second-nature. They would move about without awkwardness. Also the weapon would be instantly available. When satisfied, he directed them to the workshop outside.

Naveed was working on the vans that were near completion. He ignored the panel vans because they had no rear windows. He was concentrating on those with all round glass because they would take longer to complete.

He showed Khalid and Nazir how to make templates for each van. The window shape and size varied from one make to the next. These templates were in turn used to cut out the sticky-back transparent material to black-out the rear and side glass of each vehicle. They set about blacking out the remainder of the vans.

55.

After Fajr Prayer, Suleiman went straight to the servants' dining room for breakfast because Kabir Anwar wanted to leave early for Birmingham. His Lordship had an appointment with the Fiqh Council at the Birmingham Central Mosque on Middleway at ten-thirty.

The chauffeur had studied the map and plotted their route using 'AA Route Finder' on-line. He knew it would only take two and a half hours. He also realised that he would be travelling in the rush hour through London; the M1 and the M6, so traffic would probably be heavy throughout the entire journey. He suggested that they left at half-past-seven and his boss had readily agreed.

Once they arrived in the second largest city in the UK Suleiman switched off the navigation aid. Although was quite familiar with the route the Snooper alerted him to any hold-ups en route. It could also quickly plot an alternative route, should an accident block the road.

From past experience, the driver did not go to the main entrance of the mosque on Middleway but drove round to the large car park at the rear. Suleiman drew up at the foot of the entry steps. He climbed out of the limousine and walked round to the rear. He opened the door for his lordship. The peer stepped out and stretched.

Just then a member of the Fiqh ran down the steps. He rushed up to greet their honoured guest. The chauffeur pushed the door shut. He watched his employer move up the stairs for his meeting. He then climbed back into the driver's seat and pulled the luxury car to a parking space in the shade, at the edge of the parking lot.

Suleiman made his way to the side of the building. He let himself into the secular section of the mosque. There was a small kitchen where he could get a cup of sweetened lassi – milk with yogurt – and a snack.

Two men joined him in the queue.

"Salam Suleiman."

"Alaykumu salam Ikram."

Here stood the antithesis of a jihadi fighter. He was a clean shaven young man in a blue suit and spectacles. He looked like a successful businessman. Suleiman knew he had fought in Afghanistan as well as Syria. However, unlike many of his compatriots he moved around the world on different passports. Whenever he leaves the UK, he travels to Saudi Arabia on pilgrimage, either Hajj or

Umrah, rather than on the usual routes through Turkey. In this way he had remained below the radar of British Immigration and the Intelligence Services.

"This is my small nephew," he introduced the youngster, "Adnan Abbas. He has been accepted at university to train as a doctor. His parents are very happy. But Adnan is eighteen. He has different ideas. He wants to join us. Or travel abroad to support ISIS. He can't tell his parents. They would tell the police."

"It is good to meet you." Suleiman took his hand. "Your uncle told me all about you. You are most welcome."

Adnan stood beaming as he shook the Saudi's hand.

"The others are in the next room," Ikram interjected.

He nodded towards a door beside the counter. Then he paid for the drinks and refreshments. Suleiman followed them into the meeting room. Two more prospective fighters were waiting for their final instructions. The excitement was quite palpable as he walked into the room.

56.

Faisal went into Jo's space, once he had checked his remaining families.

"Morning ma'am."

"Good morning Faisal. I hope you have some good news. I've had a hell of a morning."

"Not sure really. Met one of my snouts and he told me that a Saudi called a meeting at Finsbury Park Mosque yesterday."

"Wasn't that where the one eye, one-armed extremist was the Imam?"

"Yes. We were simply doing surveillance in those days. But it was before 9/11, and we were naive. The powers that be, in their divine wisdom, thought it would be best to leave him alone. So we watched and observed. He corrupted a lot of young Moslems in that time. Sowed the seeds for what we've got today. All in all, a nasty piece of work."

"So?" Jo brought them back to the point. "Why the meeting?"

"This Saudi guy told them to be ready to move at a moment's notice."

"Where to?"

"He didn't know. But they will use a code-word."

"Who will?"

"The ones picking them up?"

"So the Saudi won't be picking them up?"

"Looks like," Faisal confirmed.

"So he has help. Tariq? Who is this Saudi anyway?"

"He didn't know."

"Is he from the Embassy?"

"I'll check our database for dissident Saudis."

"And, what was the code word?"

"Al Hilal?"

"What? Kosher?" She looked confused.

"No. 'Hilal' not 'halal'. It means 'Crescent Moon'. The symbol of Islam. 'Halal' actually means 'legal' or 'lawful', but it is used as an adjective with animals to explain how they are slaughtered. Like 'kosher' with the Jewish method of slaughter."

"They are the same, aren't they?" queried Jo Pullen

"Same method, different prayer," Faisal replied glibly.

"OK." Jo decided. "Check the database for 'Hilal'. Anything else?"

"No ma'am." He stood to go. "I think something big is coming."

"It's a possibility. Expect the unexpected is my motto. Let's try to get one step ahead."

The same thought went through both their minds: how could they get one step ahead when they did not even know which direction to take?

57.

Hussain brought the Land Cruiser V8 in a tight arc round the fountain and stopped. Tariq jumped out of the passenger seat and slid open the side door. His male relatives stiffly clambered out of the confines of the van relieved the journey was over. Tariq led them up the grand flight of steps to the main entrance. He heaved open the imposing double oaken doors. Ali Siddiqi led the family into the manor house. They assembled in the sitting room to discuss their plan of action.

While they were arguing the course of events, Imran and Naveed joined them. They were there to make sure the Siddiqis followed the right procedure. For although Ali wanted vengeance on his wayward daughter, it had to be in accordance with Sharia Law. If it were not, then it was murder. And Suleiman had directed that a video be made to illustrate Islamic law. It had to follow procedure.

Finally it was agreed that Tariq and Waheed would prepare Jasmine and Darren for the ritual killing. It was essential for the family to direct the punishment. They left the meeting with some sense of foreboding.

When they entered the cell, the two youngsters were still chained to their respective beds. Being in a drugged haze, they were unaware of their precarious situation.

The brothers carefully attached three huge white sheets to the wooden wine racks at the very back of the dark cellar. Then they found two simple wooden chairs. These were placed side by side in front of the sheet-covered bottle stands. They left the cellar to find the rest of the paraphernalia they needed to build the 'stage' for the execution.

Tariq returned with a large pine kitchen table, which he set about five metres in front of the chairs. Next, Waheed brought in four collapsible chairs and Tariq carried in four more. These were placed behind the table, facing the two chairs in front of the sheet. The scene was set.

With a heavy heart, Waheed unchained his sister. He pulled her legs round and put them on the floor. Then he half walked, half carried her to the right-hand chair. He tied her arms to the back of the chair, then her legs to the front legs. Her head lolled from side to side. She tried to say something, but it was very indistinct. Meanwhile, Tariq had got Darren onto the left-hand chair. Waheed tied his arms to the back of the chair while his elder brother secured his legs.

As they were finishing, the Siddiqi men filed silently into the room and arranged themselves on the chairs behind the table. Imran entered the room and laid an ornate 'L'-shaped knife scabbard on the table. It contained a decorated Jambiya, an Arabic tribal dagger, both sides of the blade of which had been carefully sharpened. They were reputed to be able to slice through sheer silk as it drifts through the air.

Meanwhile Naveed set up the camera behind the table. He squinted through the lens. He could clearly see the two drowsy figures in the chairs. He looked again and zoomed in a bit to cut out any background that might identify where they were.

Ibrahim brought round an assortment of black headscarves. These were to hide the faces of the executioners. He also carried an armful of black gowns. These had two functions; to hide their clothing thus making identification more difficult, and, to protect their clothing from blood splatter. None of the assassins must have any of the victim's DNA on them.

He gave a set of over-clothes to each member of the family. They helped each other arrange the head gear. They had to tie it in the fashion of the tribe. Also, to make sure that most of their faces were covered. It took a while for the men to feel comfortable in the traditional clothing. Finally they settled.

Tarik stood between his sister and the infidel. He nodded. Naveed zoomed into his masked face. The only things that showed were his eyes and eyebrows. He tried to keep his voice flat and unemotional. When he spoke everyone became silent. There was a palpable feeling of anticipation. Bizarrely a wave of euphoria surged amongst the silent watching men. Like the swirls of a shark in the sea.

"This Moslem girl has been a whore with this non-Moslem boy. Moslem women must not behave like prostitutes. They can't be the same as the western women. They sleep with men before they are married. This is against the law. So… in sharia law the family kill the one who brings shame on the family. In sharia law we kill the one who brings shame on the religion. Sharia law is very simple. Sharia law will make Britain great again; Great Britain with Great Sharia Law. There is only one God and his name is Allah. Allah be praised."

The last refrain rippled round the body of men.

Naveed zoomed out to bring both young people in full view. Jasmine was moving more urgently now; her head straining from side to side. Tariq moved behind her and held her shoulders firmly. She was whimpering something. It was impossible to hear what she was saying.

Darren was trying to focus on the proceedings in front of him.

Finally, Ali stood up. The chair scrapped and everyone stopped talking. He reached for the knife. He unsheathed the glinting blade. Then he walked deliberately into shot. He came from the right-hand side, to stand in front of his daughter. His son moved away to the left.

Ali hesitated, before arcing the knife in a huge semi-circle above his head. The blade glinted in the harsh neon-light of the cellar. He resembled an Old Testament Prophet. He faltered again. Then spoke with a quavering voice: "Shame on you. You brought shame on the family."

He suddenly plunged the knife through her left shoulder, from above. It plunged deep into her upper chest cavity. She screamed. He pulled the knife smoothly out. It was so sharp it slid out easily. Next he stepped up to Darren. Without hesitation, he neatly sliced the blade across his cheek. Ali's words were drowned in the high pitched scream that exploded from the boy's lips.

"You made my daughter a whore. You made her unworthy of a good Moslem man. You must die."

Ali walked to his place and sat down. Ibrahim took the weapon from his grip. He wiped the blade on a huge white sheet. Then passed it to the next man. By now the tribe had formed an orderly queue waiting their turn. They rotated in an anticlockwise direction. The white cloth soon became crimson.

Jasmine turned her head and saw Darren struggling against his bonds. Bright young blood oozing down his face from the straight-line slash make across his cheek. It was white above the line and scarlet below it. Two tone Darren. She shook her head and apologised;

"Daz," her voice cracked with emotion. "I am so sorry. What have I done to you? Poor Daz…"

She began screaming as the next thrust burned deep into her abdomen. The men of the family walked round thrice more before they were satisfied that the victims were finally quiet.

Naveed switched off the camera and took it out of the room. Tariq felt for a pulse. He shook his head and the old men filed silently out of the room.

Tariq and Waheed tore down the sheet that had acted as a backdrop to the whole drama and rolled their sister in it. All the time blood seeped through the gradually thickening swaddling cloth. Then they rolled Darren into the cloth used to wipe the knife.

On cue, Ibrahim and Khalid re-entered the room. Tariq and Waheed took each end of their sister's shroud. The other men took Darren. They processed into the back garden. A two-metre deep trench had been dug. They tossed their bundles into their makeshift graves and began unceremoniously shovelling in the damp clay soil.

There would be no tombstone. There would be no message to commemorate their short, unfinished lives. But they lay together in death, as they wished to have been in life.

58.

Faisal moved in front of Jo Pullen's desk.
"Have you got a minute?"

She was on the phone so waved him to the chair opposite. He sat and gazed at the file he had brought in.

"Well I'll get back to you, just as soon as possible... Of course... Thank you. Bye now." She hung up, "They're always collecting statistics. You'd think that these things could be collected automatically through computer-use or pre-arranged software rather than asking about things that are done and dusted. Bureaucracy. The bane of all administrative posts. Don't seek promotion. You'll asphyxiate under all the crap."

"Yes ma'am. It's why I have not sought higher status. I enjoy the streets. I don't enjoy paperwork."

"I enjoy administration. That is why I took this job. But computers were supposed to have stopped all this need to store hard copies. What happened to that plan about saving the forests? Sorry. I will stop ranting. Deep breath. So... what can I do for you?"

"I have just got the report from Mervin and Jackie," he informed her.

"They are shadowing Lord Anwar," Jo clarified.

"Yep. Well they're in Birmingham. He went there to attend a meeting in the mosque. He's still there."

"And..."

"I researched 'Al Hilal' and came up with something interesting,"

"Really?" She waited patiently for him to enlighten her.

"Lord Anwar's boat is called 'Crescent Moon'. Maybe we should be watching that instead."

"I can't get any more personnel," she pointed out.

"What if we took our guys off the house and sent them to Brighton instead. I think that would be more beneficial. More relevant to our investigation."

"Brighton?"

"Yep. 'Crescent Moon' is moored in the marina there."

"Does he use the boat much?"

"A few times a month he swans off to France or the Channel Isles for lunch or a meeting."

"How the other half lives…" Jo lamented.

"I was thinking, with the 'Hilal' connection, we should perhaps concentrate our limited resources on that very connection, rather than a more general one."

"I like it. The Hilal connection is the only clue we have. Transfer Mervin's team to Brighton."

"Good. I'll get on it right away."

For the first time since the disappearance of Tarik and Khalid, Faisal was feeling more positive. However, he was aware that it was the only lead that they had. But it was a bit tenuous at best. He crossed his fingers. Then when he sat down, he crossed his toes as well. Now he was back at his work station, moving their agents seemed a bit dramatic. He hoped he was right. This could cost lives. It could cost him his job…

59.

The Fajr Prayer call echoed eerily through the corridors of Gayhurst Manor. There were more than the usual stirrings this Wednesday morning. The whole Siddiqi tribe had slept over. They had been emotionally exhausted by the ordeals of the previous twenty-four hours. However, they all converged on the washroom at the end of the corridor. The floor was very wet when they had finished. After prayer, they trouped into the dining room for breakfast.

Ibrahim fried omelette served with plenty of chapattis and roti bread. This was washed down with lassi, sherbet or green tea. There were fresh mangos, bananas, apples and slices of melon in bowls in the middle of their long table. The elders enjoyed the male comradery and the shared food. The stresses and blame of yesterday was put on the back burner. They were in fine fettle when they gathered for the Sun Rise Prayer.

As soon as the prayer was over they went out to the white Land Cruiser. This time Hussain was accompanied by Waheed in the front of the van.

He wanted to say goodbye to his extended family.

60.

Shami Shah returned to his two-bedroomed apartment after attending Sun Rise Prayer at the Finsbury Park Mosque. As he opened the door, he knew someone had already entered his living space. This intuition had developed since he had lived in a war zone. He had somehow developed a sixth sense. He reasoned that it was a heightened self-preservation instinct. It was something that might keep him alive for a little longer.

He stepped into the flat. He leaned his back against the door and listened. He stood very still until he heard breathing. They were long, even breaths; so the person was relaxed, not nervous and ready to spring. He moved round the flat, keeping to the walls, like a rat on a food foray.

The living room and kitchen were clear. He picked up a carving knife from the scullery drawer en route. It was held outstretched in front of him. He checked behind his bedroom door. Then the wardrobe and bathroom. So there was only his brother's room left.

He pushed the door with his foot and came in low. No one was lurking behind the door. His brother was sprawled across the bed, still in the clothes he had worn the day before.

Shami stepped backwards out of the room. He went into the kitchen and put the carving knife away. He filled the kettle and put it on to boil. Then went into the bathroom and turned on the cold tap. While the bath was filling he stripped off most of his clothes until he stood in his underpants. There were several scars disfiguring his lean torso and left leg. He had been injured in a bomb blast from a British plane. He had also been shot twice. His body may have been scarred but it was also very wiry, without an ounce of fat. When the bath was half full he turned off the tap and returned to Sahid's room.

Without warning, Shami grabbed his younger brother's hair. He yanked him off the bed. He dragged him across the floor gathering rugs on the way. Sahid was screaming loudly and clawing at the hand that was clamped firmly to his head. When they reached the bathtub, Shami heaved his younger brother up. Then used his own body weight to tumble him into the water. It sloshed onto the floor. He rammed his younger brother's head under the water. Sahid thrashed and splashed as the elder sibling counted to five. Then pulled him up for a breath of precious air. He counted five and ducked him again. He slowly counted five and pulled the head up again. This time only long enough for a lungful of air. He ducked him down again.

When Sahid began to choke and his body convulsed, Shami allowed him to collapse onto the rumpled pile of rugs. He lay, spluttering and coughing up water.

Finally the younger man was able to pull himself to his feet and began shouting incoherently at the calm figure of his older brother. Shami handed him a towel. Sahid stripped off and rubbed himself down, shouting all the time,

"You are mad…mad. You could have… could have killed me…. What did you do that for? You are a crazy… Crazy man… Do you hear me? Uhh? Crazy fool…"

Shami let the accusations flow until Sahid began to shake uncontrollably. Then he grabbed both his young brother's ears. The words stopped. He pulled the face close to his own. The young man had gone quiet, staring unblinking into his brother's snake like eyes.

"If you ever take drugs again I will kill you."
"What do…" Sahid was mildly defensive.
"I followed you. I saw where you went. Next time we go there it is to kill those devils. Do you understand?"
"Yes." Sahid was shocked at the vehemence in his brother's voice.
"We will go together, you and me. They are animals. We will split their throats like we slit the throat of a sheep at Eide. Do you understand?"
"Yes." Sahid was very subdued and Shami released his ears.
"Now get some dry clothes on. I will make you a hot drink. Then I am going to arrange for us to kill the animals. And… and you… you my brother… you will slit the throat of your enemies. It is time for you to grow up.

No more your mother's baby. Now you must become your father's son."

Sahid said nothing. He rubbed his head where the hair had been all but pulled from his scalp. It burned and his whole body throbbed. But his mind was clear. He was in a state of shock. He could not imagine killing anybody like that.

Suddenly the ideal of martyrdom appeared much less attractive.

61.

Mervin Cato and Jackie Montgomery drove their unmarked vehicle into the Marina. They parked in the reserved spaces for residents, by the jetty gate. Mervin took out a key which let them onto the concourse. They walked all the way to Reception at the end of West Jetty. It was busy with several yachtsmen booking themselves out in the fine weather.

Eventually Sharon Smith, the marina receptionist, introduced herself. They explained that they had rented a boat for two weeks and were not sure where it was berthed. She got them to fill out the forms and pay a deposit for the keys and a temporary visitor's pass to the marina. Then she led them back along West Jetty until the transect to East Jetty. Their boat was tied up alongside the second intersecting jetty on the left, number 32, in the third berth backing onto the water.

Sharon explained that 'Dreamland' was a Dyna Craft 58 with Twin Detroit 92 engines. It could cruise at 16 knots and speed at 24. She explained the workings of the galley. Then she showed them the pumps. Sharon explained that they had to be operated at least once every twenty-four hours. She took great pains to point out that most damage was done when owners or tenants forgot to pump out the bilges. They shot a quick glance at each other and nodded that they understood.

Once she finally left, Mervin went to park the car nearer to their actual jetty. He also collected the bags while Jackie began to explore the cabins. Although she respected Mervin's experience, she had no intention of sleeping in the same room, let alone the same bed. To her relief, there were two state bedrooms, each with ensuite facilities and gigantic double beds. She wished Jonny, her partner, could come and join them. Sighing she returned to the flybridge at the back of the vessel to see if she could see the suspect's vessel.

It did not take her long to identify 'Crescent Moon'. It was a much bigger craft than theirs. It was berthed with the bigger ocean-going vessels alongside Jetty number 31. It was in the seventh berth. There appeared to be no activity on board. In fact as she looked round at the other boats, most seemed empty.

She wondered what yachtsmen and women did when they were aboard. It must be like a caravan holiday, she decided, but without the ablution block or the kiddies' play area. By arranging a deck chair under the canopy on the aft deck, she had a very good view of the other boat, without looking too obvious.

When Mervin arrived with the luggage, they went below to unpack. They had to get themselves comfortable for yet another long, drawn out surveillance. It was an activity or rather inactivity they were both very familiar with. On their employment contracts they were classified as MSOs or Mobile Surveillance Officer. The in-house joke was that ninety percent of the time they were in fact ISOs – Immobile Surveillance Officers. However, they had to agree that this was certainly one of the most comfortable.

"Like being in a luxury hotel," Suggested Mervin, "Paid for by the tax-payer."

62.

As soon as the security barrier rose, Suleiman drove into the square driveway in front of Westminster Palace. He pulled over and climbed out of the limousine. He walked round to the rear door. Lord Anwar strode into the building.   He was clutching his document bag with a bearing of some importance.   But the car did not move immediately.

Suleiman switched on his phone. Sure enough there was a voice message from Shami.   The British-Pakistani explained all about Sahid.   He promised that they both wanted to punish the drug dealers.

To give himself time to think Suleiman hung up and changed his SIM card. He realised that they could pick up all the Finsbury Park Mujahedeen in one fell swoop. Although he thought it would alert the authorities that they were beginning a big operation. Especially so soon after they had collected both tagged veterans from Brixton.

But under the circumstances, they had to do it now, because of Shami's predicament.   If the Syrian veteran took things into his own hands, it might endanger his entire plan.   Also, now Imran had promised that the weapons could be ready in a couple of days, everything was falling into place. And one thing about Suleiman's plan was that it had to be flexible. It had to react to external changes. It now looked like everything would be ready sooner than planned. Therefore it was time to collect the fighters.

He returned Shami's call.   The Saudi verified that the British Pakistanis would be picked up later that day. He also confirmed that they would make an example of the drug dealers.   Then all return to Gayhurst Manor.   But from that moment until the transport actually arrived, he was to make sure there would be no surprises.

Suleiman stressed that he did not want his long awaited planned attack threatened. He liked the idea of the filming the execution of drug dealers. Maintaining it would assist their claims that Sharia Law punishes wrongdoers. But he did not want a revenge party to interfere with the Planned Attack. It must not jeopardise the Big Plan.

Once they had agreement, he hung up and took out the SIM card. He put the old one in his left pocket and placed a new one in the phone.

Suleiman called the Manor and spoke to Naveed. He instructed him to pick up the rest of the Finsbury Park contingent that afternoon. Ibrahim was to drive a second vehicle with Khalid, Nazir and Tarik all of whom should be fully armed.

The Saudi emphasised that Ibrahim should carry his video recorder. They had to bring some Jambiyas to execute the drug dealers. He hoped that the resulting video could be released along with the execution of Jasmine. That being the case he suggested that Tarik introduce it, in the same way he did with the first one. It would give a better impression of all these things being planned. That, he felt would compound the impact.

Naveed suggested it would be better done at two in the morning. He said that defences are down in the cold light of predawn. His experience in battlefield skirmishes showed that just before dawn was the best time to attack an enemy. When it was at its lowest ebb.

Furthermore, he argued, there would be fewer people about to witness or interfere with the task in hand. Suleiman agreed and they broke the connection. He removed the card and put it in his left pocket. He slipped in another new card. He rang Shami to explain when the pickup was to be and why. He also instructed him to contact Salman so he would be ready on time. The SIM card joined the others.

Then he turned the ignition key. The limousine purred into life. He accelerated towards the security barrier under the shadow of Westminster Palace. After the security police took a brief look into the rear of the vehicle, he was waved through. He turned left into the flow crawling past Westminster Abbey.

63.

Hussain dropped the Siddiqi family at 'Jamia Masjid', a mosque in the centre of Bradford. In that way they could go back to their individual families without attracting too much attention. If they had been delivered individually, neighbours might remember. They were already thinking about their alibis.

Waheed bade a fond farewell to his father and uncles. He had gained some control of his emotions during the journey. He had taken part in the execution of his sister. That changed everything. Nothing could ever be the same again. The childhood he had known was gone. It had washed away with his sister's blood. Once that act was completed, he could not go back. All the scenarios were too horrible to contemplate. The whole family had been involved with the brutal murder of his sister. If they were wrong, that was murder. But it was their religion, so it was right. That was the conclusion he had come to. While rooted to the seat in the van, unable to go anywhere, he was forced to think it through.

During the journey north he had come to terms with his fate. Now he was ready to die for his religion. Nothing else made sense after what they had done. He returned to the white van with dry eyes.

They pulled away from the terrace houses in Howard Street, returning to the M26, and the road to his destiny.

64.

Jo called Faisal, Malcolm and David Jones into her office. "OK. Anything to report?" she invited.

"Mervin and Jackie are aboard 'Dreamland' in Brighton Marina," Davy reported.

"Good. What did they say?"

"All is quiet aboard the 'Crescent Moon' at the moment," He confirmed.

"Now that the police have finished searching the absentee's homes," Jo informed them. "We can put the surveillance gear back. That way we will be the first to know when… or indeed if… they return."

"Did the police come up with anything?" Faisal wanted to know.

"No. They are still talking to neighbours and workmates. They are trying to find anyone who knows where their extended families are living in UK. But it is all so time-consuming… that's why we involved them in the first place."

"They have their uses," Faisal observed.

Malcolm brought them up to date. "Tom Canning has tested all the recording devices and repaired or replaced where necessary."

"Good," said Faisal. "We lost visuals in Tariq's hallway four months ago… and the audio in Khalid's bedroom six weeks ago."

"Well… hopefully," Jo added, "we will have everything up and running in a couple of hours."

"If there is anyone there," Davy added unnecessarily.

"Malcolm," Jo ignored him, "Collect the refurbished electronics from Tom. Then you and Davy can reinstall them. And… come to think about it, see if the electrician's van is available. Just in case they suddenly return. At least you've got a foot to stand on."

"OK ma'am," Malcolm acknowledged.

"And Faisal. Just check though our other Asbos, once more. Make sure no one else has done a runner since we last checked. And... and then you and Tom stand by so Malcolm can check that everything is working before they leave each premise. Then at least we can start with one hundred percent coverage."

"Fine."

"Any questions? No? OK. Off you go."

Tom Canning sat at Faisal's station all afternoon retuning his receiver to pick up clear signals. First they replaced the devices round Tarik's home. Remotely they watched Malcolm and Davy going round the house. Painstakingly, they tested the microphones, as well as the hidden cameras.

Then the whole process was repeated when they were in Khalid's apartment. Eventually, Faisal declared that they were all working well. They had put two more cameras in both properties to give themselves more time if they tampered with them again. Malcolm and Davy were told to stand down.

Tom went back to his work station near the main entrance. Faisal made contact with Mervin to see if there were any developments in Brighton. They had nothing to report.

Wednesday was turning out to be a nuts-and-bolts day. Faisal was beginning to feel frustrated again. It was the most difficult thing about their job. So much of their time was spent waiting for something to happen. As he was fond of saying:

"I'm not so much a Man of Action; I am a Man of Inaction."

65.

Once Hussain and Waheed had returned to Gayhurst Manor, Ibrahim called a meeting. He said that the video of Jasmine's execution had been dubbed onto a new film. He said it was good. In that it would show Sharia Law at its best. He went on to explain that they were going to pick up the Finsbury Park Mujahedeen in the early hours of the morning. They would be making another video to put out with the first. In preparation for their ordeal, he would prepare an early evening meal. Then they needed to go to bed very early. They should get as much rest as possible.

He delegated jobs to be completed before they went out. Naveed was to make sure the white Land Cruiser and the Ford Transit, with the side-bench seats, were full of fuel. He was to check that the oil and water levels were good. Also look at the tyre pressures.

Imran was to arm Tariq and Waheed. He must allow them to practice with their revolvers. He wanted them ready for the battle ahead.

Hussain was to sharpen both edges of their three Jambiyas. Then he was to recharge both video camera batteries. He wanted them ready to use. The whole point of this trip was to film the execution of drug dealers. Thus illustrating the justice of Islamic Law.

Then Ibrahim returned to the kitchen. He wanted to be sure that they had a good meal before they went to bed. He began by baking several fresh loaves of bread. Then Ibrahim went about cutting up fresh vegetables for a nourishing stew. The fighters needed their energy for the night ahead.

66.

Jackie settled down for a catnap while Mervin kept watch. There had been no movement on the 'Crescent Moon'. After many years of surveillance duty he had learned patience. Even when Section was on his back for results, he maintained his calm exterior. He could get edgy deep down, but he never let it show.

Faisal had just been in contact, asking for an update yet again. It was just this kind of pressure he resented. The reality was that someone was pressing Faisal for answers.

But that was not his concern. He was the man in the field. He was at the sharp end. It was his life on the line.

Mervin literally shrugged it off. He settled himself into a less conspicuous position. He had moved an armchair up to the flybridge. No point in being uncomfortable on a stake out. He had to look to all intents and purposes like a tourist. He had to give the impression of someone relaxing in the sunshine.

Two hours later, Jackie emerged from the state room carrying two mugs of coffee. She placed one on the deck near his feet. He was always amazed at how quickly she was refreshed. His wife needed eight hours or she was a real bitch the following morning. That was why he liked being partnered with Jackie. She was one hundred percent professional. He wondered if she ever imagined them sleeping together on a job like this. The facilities were excellent. Then he remembered to share the text message, "Faisal texted for an update."

"Has anything happened?"

"Nope. Same old, same old," he told her.

"Do you want to knock on their door?"

"It had crossed my mind," he admitted.

"You could use our trusted electrical company overalls method."

"OK. Then we will know if we are watching an empty boat or not."

As soon as he raised himself, she jumped into it, slopping her coffee on the deck.

"You only said that so you could get my chair," he accused her.

"Too right," she shot back.

Fifteen minutes later he was wandering along Jetty 31, clipboard in hand. He was wearing the *BDF Electrical* black fleece with an orange collar. To help authenticate his errand he started with the first boat on the north side of the transect jetty. He knocked on the cabin roofs and waited for an answer. When no one responded he would move to the next. Finally he reached the 'Crescent Moon'.

Mervin walked up the gangplank. He ducked under the canvas fly-deck canopy and jumped lightly onto the deck. Unlike on their vessel, this canopy was solid. As he straightened, a man emerged through the sliding glass door. He was dressed in a long grey and white striped dishdasha and small lacy Kufi Topi.

"What do you want?" He spoke with a strong Arabic accent.

"Ahh! I am from the marine owners. I am checking electrical meters. Are you having any problems?"

"No problem. Now you go," Although not threatening, the man stepped forward, blocking any forward movement.

"Can I read your meter?" Mervin noticed a second figure lurking behind the glinting glass door.

"All meters on the jetty," The stranger moved nearer Mervin. It caused him to step backwards.

"Of course. But have you got any electrical meters on board?"

"No. Now go."

"Thank you so much. I will just..." Mervin stepped onto the gangplank and beat a hasty retreat to the jetty side. He continued visiting boats, in case they were watching. He wanted to continue the fantasy, to make them think he was genuine.

"Did you see his shoes?" Abdulaziz asked.

"No."

"Clean. Highly polished. Expensive. Not a workman's shoes."

"Now I think of it," Rahman added, "He did not check the meters on the jetty when he left."

"We must tell Suleiman. It could be the police or government security." Abdulrahman looked worried.

"How did they find us?" Wondered Abdulaziz. "We must be very careful. They may be watching us."

67.

Tom Canning left Thames House and walked along Millbank between the Palace of Westminster and the Abbey, then turned right on Bridge Street, under the shadow of Big Ben. He crossed the road and followed the Victoria Embankment.

He loved London on a bustling weekday during rush hour. It gave him a feeling of safety, being lost in a throng. He wondered if it were how the wildebeest felt when crossing the Masai Mara in Kenya. He'd been on safari with Emily, who he was about to meet.

Maybe the African connection was triggered by meeting her again. It had been over a year since they had lived together. She had moved to Cheltenham, to be nearer her work and he stayed in Haywards Heath. Then she simply was not there anymore and time passed. He was not even sure if they still had a relationship.

He turned north at the Embankment tube station, onto Villiars Street. He pushed against the flood of people migrating the other way. Then he reached *The Prince of Wales* public house on the right. This was where they used to meet before catching the train from Charring Cross. The pub looked the same. Several people were smoking behind a makeshift fabric barrier to separate them from the hordes of passers-by. He was feeling nervous.

Inside was dark after the evening sun. She was not in the window space where they often used to sit. He moved through the crowd between the bar and the tables. The bar with its strangely modern wire gantry of glinting polished glasses was on the right. While on the left, the tables lined the dark dull green wall. It was crowded. Every seat appeared to be taken. He began scanning round again. Then he spied her.

She was tucked into a corner, on a small round table, almost touching the man next to her. Tom breathed in deeply and went towards the table. She looked up and smiled as he approached. She was a plain looking woman. Then her face lit up as she smiled and he felt something flip inside him.

"Long time no see," She said gaily.

"Yes. It is."

He leaned awkwardly over the table to kiss her and connected with her chin. She kissed his nose. They hastily pulled apart.

"Want a drink?"

He asked. She touched her full glass of white wine. He nodded and smiled.

Tom went to the bar and asked for a pint of *Peroni*. He paid. He lifted the tall thin glass and sipped. He meandered his way through the crowd back to the table. Then lowered himself onto a short round stool. Tom overflowed it in all directions. He was crammed between the table and the wooden partition boxing off the door to the toilet, downstairs in the cellar.

"Clement weather," she ventured.

"Indeed," he agreed, "How's it been going?"

"Busy as always. Been put in charge of the Russian Department. It restarted after the recent Ukraine fiasco. Looks like we underestimated them after the Cold War ended."

"Yes. That's good. You speak Russian. It will be good for your career. Oh yes... I've been moved too... to the Syrian Desk."

"You can't speak Arabic or Farsi. You only speak French and German."

"I know," he agreed. "They are using my computer skills. I'm now a Digital Intelligence Tactical Solutions Developer. I'm too fat to be a spook."

"You're not fat, you're cuddly. My cuddly geek. You are too nice to be a spook anyway."

"Erm... thanks." He had missed having Emily's support all these months. She made him feel good about himself. She always said that he suffered from low-self-esteem.

"You'll like that. Fiddling with gadgets. You always liked your boy's toys. Perhaps you should have come with me to GCHQ?"

"Oh yes! That reminds me. Talking of GCHQ, it's because of that I asked you to meet me." As he stretched his legs to get more comfortable on the short stool, he kicked her little overnight bag under the table.

"I see," she said.

He gave her the memory stick and explained the problem. When he finished, she stood to go saying,

"Looks like we have finished our business." She reached down for the bag.

"Erm. I thought we might do something," He had to stop her disappearing… again.

"What?"

"A meal… erm… for old time's sake." She sat down again as he continued. "If you stayed for a meal, maybe… erm… you could stay for the… erm… whole night."

Emily's face lit up. "The whole night! Wow. You know how to woo a girl."

"I mean in Haywards Heath." He was struggling to be understood.

"That's what I hoped."

"We can go upstairs to the *Rudyard Kipling*… erm… for a bite, then erm… home."

He finished lamely. She touched her half-empty glass and added, "Mine's a medium white wine."

68.

Hussain swung the leading van into Stroud Green Road. It was just after three in the morning. He drove under the complicated railway bridge system. Then turned first right into Woodstock Road. They stopped outside a four-storey Victorian terraced house backing onto the railway embankment.

He and Tariq got out of the van. They walked through an opening in the wall where a gate used to be. Hussain stepped to the side of the stairs to the front door. He went down to the basement flat.

Tariq drew his pistol as Hussain knocked lightly on the door. Soon a light came on. Salman Pervez opened the door. His huge handlebar moustache looked somewhat dishevelled.

"Al Hilal," Hussain began, "We have..."

Salman put his finger to his lips and beckoned them in. They tip-toed inside and the older man said out loud,

"No. He doesn't live here," While closing the door loudly.

They tip-toed in to the bedroom. It smelt of unwashed male bodies. There was someone sleeping in one of the beds. His snoring resounded round the room. Salman sat on the side of the bed. He gently shook the sleeper's shoulder. A wide-eyed face appeared from the bedclothes. Salman looked into Amir's scared rabbit eyes. He placed his finger over his mouth. Then waved his other hand at the two strangers standing near the door.

Without a word the two men dressed. They put a few possessions into a canvas holdall. As they gathered their possessions Hussain collected their mobile phones, watches and the iPad. He took out the batteries and slipped everything into his multi-pocketed holdall.

Ten minutes later they emerged from the flat. The four men climbed aboard the van. As Hussain pulled away from the kerb, a second van followed close behind.

The next stop was at the Shah brother's home. This time it was Ibrahim and Waheed in the second van that went into the flat. Within ten minutes Shami and Sahid were aboard. The small convoy drove along Seven Sisters Road then turned right into Queen's Drive. They took the first on the left until they came to a apartment block complex. They drove through the open wrought iron gates and into the parking area.

There were no vacant slots so Hussain reversed on to the pavement, just inside the gate on the right. Ibrahim drove to the other end of the parking zone. There were no spaces so he pulled the van onto a dry, dusty flowerbed.

Ten minutes later Sahid was knocking on his dealer's door. Nothing stirred. He stepped aside. Ibrahim and Hussain placed two long handled jemmy bars into the left hand doorjamb. One at the top and one near the bottom. They were joined by helping hands to pull the bars towards the wall. With the splintering sound of tearing wood, the whole door fitting was levered outwards from its brick surround.

Ibrahim and Hussain heaved it far enough for the armed jihadists to move stealthily into the dark flat. They followed, pulling the door frame over the gap as best they could.

Without a sound, the five occupants of the flat were quickly gagged and marched into the sitting room. Ibrahim arranged a line of five chairs along the wall. Tariq and Waheed tied the victim's hands behind them and their legs to the chair. In the same way they had bound Jasmine and Darren before. Hussain arranged the camera in the middle of the room. The bewildered dealers watched preparations over their gags.

Ibrahim gave out the black thobes and ghutrahs to the executioners. Now, as the invaders began to dress up like Mujahedeen, the flatmates began to mumble behind their gags. They began to fidget in their bonds. They had been busted before. Although this had been different, in that the 'police' were silent, they were not afraid. It was just another police raid. An occupational hazard when in the drugs trade. Even though they had been trussed up like Christmas turkeys, they still expected to be taken to the nearest police station. Now it was beginning to look somewhat different. As sleep fell away, reality kicked in. It hit home suddenly. Two of the dealers began to struggle to free themselves.

Five masked figures, dressed in black from head to foot, lined up behind the seated figures. Each of them carried a curved knife. They took charge of the victim they were standing behind. Those who had been struggling were unceremoniously hit on the top of the head with the knife handle. It hurt and stilled the unrest.

Tariq moved in front of the line of chairs. He began his spiel in English. As it progressed, the gagged heads began to move around more frantically.

"These infidels sold drugs to a Moslem so they must die. This is Shariah Law. I have listened to many English people complaining. They say that the police do nothing about the gangs of drug dealers that are corrupting young people. When England has Shariah Law you will be safe from these animals. They will be eliminated from the gene pool. There is only one God and his name is Allah. Allah is great."

He moved behind the camera. The executioners tore the gags off simultaneously. The captives were screaming their innocence. Each black shape slapped the prisoner in front of them on the head until they were quiet. They looked dully at the camera.

Sahid stepped forward with his back to the camera. This was so he could not be identified later. He showed his face to the prisoners. They knew exactly who he was. He had been so bad, he had slept over. They sold him some good skag from the new batch that arrived in the morning. He was an ungrateful nark. They would kill him for this. They looked up at him sullenly.

"You sold me some smack." They protested loudly so were hit again. "Yesterday I stayed here because I could not move. You took all my money. You made me unclean so I couldn't go to the mosque. You must die for this. There is only one God and his name is Allah."

Three of the jihadists revealed their knives. With little preamble they slit the throat of the person in front of them. They squealed like stuck pigs. The other two victims could not comprehend what they had just witnessed. Two knives were passed to the last two executioners. They acted quickly. The last of the prisoners began gasping as the first expired.

The black shapes turned to the right and walked out of shot in single file. Hussain waited for the last victim to finish squirming then switched off the camera.

The executioners took off their robes and headscarves then returned them to Hussain. He stuffed them into a black holdall. They must leave no evidence to trace anything back to them.

They surrendered their knives to Ibrahim who wrapped them in a red towel. This was put in the bag with the clothing. With remarkable solemnity, they walked silently past the victims. Then out of the flat and down to the vans.

Hussain and Ibrahim carried the bag of used equipment out of the broken door. They placed it on the ground then propped the door, still in its frame, back into the aperture.

If you walked past the door, you could tell there was damage. As they were known drug dealers, no one would interfere.

Speed was of the essence now.

They followed their comrades down to the transport.

69.

Faisal carried his bike into the lift. This morning was humid. Sweat beaded his brow. Cycling had been hard work. He was looking forward to his shower. After which, he took the lift to the third floor. Then stepped briskly to the last door on the right. He knocked and was greeted by the Forsyth twins in their male personas.
"Good morning Francis. Hi Michael. Sticky day." Faisal gazed into the eye scanner.
"Good morning Mr Khan," chirped Francis. "Indeed it is."

The door slid open and he turned as the semi-circular door swished round him. Like always he turned on his computer and went for a coffee. But he was interrupted when David called him over.
"I want you to listen to this." Davy handed Faisal the earphones.
"I can't hear anything."
"I know. There were some strange noises in the night," David reported.

"What kind of noises?"

"Muffled. Like people creeping about not wanting to be heard."

"Oh my God," exclaimed Faisal. "We haven't got another runner, have we?"

"It has never been this quiet. Salman always goes to pray. You know, predawn and dawn. The lot. This is the first time he has ever missed. In fact…" He shrugged.

"We've got another one." Faisal stood up and addressed the room. "Listen everyone. Looks like we have another Asbo playing truant. Check all the Syrians and report any silences. Let's have it ready for our beloved project manager when she gets in."

He rushed over to his computer and began scanning through all the audios, at the same time monitoring the videos.

"Faisal." It was Davy again. "Another one from Finsbury Park."

"OK. Everyone. Keep scanning. We need to know the exact number."

Thirty minutes later Josephine Pullen walked into the office with a huge grin across her face. It did not stay there long.

"Morning Ma'am." Faisal spoke as she passed his work station. "Got some bad news I'm afraid."

"Not another runner?" She smiled broadly.

"Yes. How did you know?"

"I didn't." The smile had gone, "I don't believe it. How many this time?"

"Same as last. Two guys disappeared from Brixton on Sunday, and now, four days later, two go from Finsbury Park."

"We need to know if they've taken anything." She looked haunted, "We need to check the accommodation."

"I've taken the liberty of sending Malcolm and Davy," Faisal said carefully, "They left fifteen minutes ago."

"Well done," Jo wiped her brow. "You did right. Tell them to strip out all our bugs. Then call the local police to try and find out where they've gone. See if they have left a trail…"

"I also took the liberty of contacting 'Dreamland'," Faisal elaborated. "You know… Mervin's ship."

"Any activity there?"

"None whatsoever. They made contact yesterday and…"

"They did what?" Jo was frowning.

"Mervin pretended to be an electrician and visited the 'Crescent Moon'. There are at least two crew. Both dressed in traditional Arabic clothes. But they never seem to appear on deck."

"I didn't authorise him to make contact," Jo said menacingly, "I hope he didn't cock it up."

Faisal flinched as she clacked over to her work space. He had been praised for taking the initiative about following up on the absentees. Then spoken severely to because

Mervin had tried to find out if anyone were aboard the boat. He got back to monitoring his Asbos.

70.

Suleiman waited for the security bar to rise. Then drove into the drop-off point in front of the Palace of Westminster. Lord Anwar was due to speak at a debate about renewable energy in the afternoon.

Whenever he had an afternoon debate, he always arrived in the morning. It gave him time to run through his speech. He could check with colleagues for any changes to expect to the agenda. It also put him in the right frame of mind.

He was exceedingly proud to be a member of the House of Lords. He took his duties extremely seriously. Regarding it as a way of helping integrate his people into this wonderfully flexible society.

Meanwhile his chauffeur was following a very different agenda. He pushed the rear door shut and walked round to the driver's seat. As always, as soon as his lordship was out of the car, he switched on his 'car' phone and waited. There were two calls; one from Gayhurst Manor and the other from the 'Crescent Moon'. He called the manor first.

"Salam-o-al-aikum Naveed. How are you?"
"Alaykumu salam Suleiman. I am fine. How are you?"

"I am good. What did you want to say?"

"All our guests have arrived safely. And the film was made successfully."

"Al-ham-dulillah. I will be there in about ninety minutes. Hopefully, I can see both videos."

"We look forward to seeing you. Travel in peace."

"Stay in peace." And Suleiman hung up. He changed the SIM card before dialling the boat.

"Salam-o-alaikum Abdulaziz," he had recognised the captain's voice. "How are you?"

"Alaykumu salam Suleiman. I am fine. How are you?"

"Alhamdulillah. Everything is going well. What is your news?"

"Yesterday we had a visitor."

"What kind of visitor?" Suleiman could feel the hairs on his neck raising.

"He said he was checking the electricity."

"Checking the electricity? There are meters on the quay. It is not necessary."

"Rahman told him and he seemed surprised. His shoes were too good for a British workman. His voice was too British for a black man. He was not what he was pretending to be."

Suleiman felt a cold shadow cross his inner being.

Then Abdulaziz asked, "What shall we do?"

"You must stay on the yacht. But tomorrow Lord Anwar wants to go to Jersey."

"We will need more provisions."

"OK. But leave it to the last moment. And switch on the cameras so we know if anyone has been on board."

"God willing everything will be alright."

"God willing. But do not leave the boat. And... maybe... you had better scan it for bugs now..."

"Alhamdulillah. We did that last night after we thought about who he might be. Everything is clean."

"Alhamdulillah. Thanks be to God. You did well. I will bring his lordship about ten, tomorrow morning."

"Salam-o-alaikum. See you tomorrow, God willing."

"Alaykumu salam. Yes. God willing."

71.

"I think we are all here," The Controller observed. "Let's start with the current situation regarding the disappearing tagged Syrian returnees... Jo?"

"Thank you, sir. Well, it looks like at least eight people disappeared on Sunday from the south London region and at least three more from north London, on... erm...on Wednesday, that is yesterday."

"How many were tagged?" interrupted Raymond Mingdon.

"I'm coming to that, if you'd let me finish." Jo frowned. "The whole Siddiqi family disappeared. But it is only Tariq and his younger brother, Waheed that we are really worried about. Then there is Khalid Ahmad, who like Tariq was tagged, and his cousin, Nazir Bashirn, who was not tagged, disappeared from Finsbury Park..."

"There has been increased 'chatter' on the social media networks," began Ray. "But not an exceptional amount. GCHQ do not seem perturbed by it."

"Well," began Jo. "We feel perturbed," She threw a look at Ray Mingdon, "Very perturbed. We feel that it is significant that two tagged Syrian veterans and two more potential fighters have suddenly disappeared."

The Controller wanted to know more. "Apart from the fact that they have unexpectedly vanished, which is remarkable in itself... is there anything else that supports your feelings of an increased threat?"

"No sir. But the disappearance alone is enough for us to advise you to go onto an increased threat of terrorist attack alert," Jo suggested.

"I'm inclined to..."

The Controller was interrupted by a loud rap at the door and without preamble one of the techies wheeled in a TV monitor on an AVA trolley on spinning castors.

"Sorry to interrupt you sir. But Tom Canning felt that you had to see this."

Sky News was on. Every eye was focussed on the image of someone talking to camera. The caption announcing a jihadist execution in Finsbury Park. The technician turned up the volume, arranged the cables, then left. The room fell silent while they tried to hear what was going on, then someone asked,

"How do they know it was an execution?"

"Is this connected to the disappearance of our guys in the area?" someone else asked.

162

"You mean Khalid and Nazir?" asked Jo.

The Controller raised his hand and spoke, "OK. OK. We need to find out exactly what's going on here. We're going to have an interval of... erm... thirty minutes." Picking up the phone he said, "I need to speak to someone in New Scotland Yard and Counter Terrorism about the reported Islamists executions in Finsbury Park as soon as possible." And he hung up, before continuing. "OK. Return to your sections and find out all you can about these attacks. Also, see if you can find out about why these people are disappearing now. Why now? Report back here in thirty minutes. OK off you go."

And he strode purposefully out of the room.

72.

On arriving at the manor, Suleiman climbed out of the Bentley and stretched. He had not slept well the night before. As they got nearer the time of attack, his imagination conjured up different scenarios. His imagination took over. Everything, as far as he was concerned, was pure fantasy. He would be glad when these years of preparation were finally over. Naveed came from securing the gates to greet the chauffeur.

"Salam-o-alaikum." Naveed walked forward with outstretched hand.

"Alaykumu salam." Suleiman took the proffered hand. Then they touched right cheeks together. As they entered the garage, they were still holding hands.

"We need to convert the last two vans," Naveed pointed out.

"Mafi mushkila." Suleiman could see no problem. "Start them immediately. We can use the Land Cruiser to pick up the Birmingham fighters."

"Alhamdulillah." Then Naveed turned to Tariq. "OK. Finish that off for now and bring in one of the new vans. Cut off the roof, like I showed you."

Tariq nodded then went back to help his brother finish the spraying.

"Now show me the films," Suleiman said eagerly, "The release should be timed before our attack to show everyone that we mean business."

"Come this way." Naveed led him towards the big house. When they walked into the lounge, Suleiman sat in front of the huge TV while Naveed went to his room for the DVDs.

Upon his return, he switched on the TV and put the small silver disc into the player. However, before he could press 'Play' their attention was caught by what was on TV. Aljazeera News focussed in and dominated the screen. There was a reporter outside the apartment block in Finsbury Park, north London, interviewing tenants about what happened the night before.

"Alhamdulillah." Naveed praised the Lord that the deaths were gaining international recognition. They listened in silence to the statement from the police spokesman, who confirmed that the victims; two women and three men, had had their throats cut. Therefore the police understood it to be a copy-cat Islamist State killing.

"They will find out soon enough that it is not 'copy-cat'," Suleiman declared.

"Furthermore," the reporter continued, "police had recovered a large amount of cash, a huge stash of class 'C' drugs and a significant amount of class 'A' drugs they could not rule out a rival drugs gang killing them to take over their territory." The report concluded: "In fact at this stage of the investigation, the police are keeping an open mind as to the actual motive. But they are appealing to any members of the public who might know something that could help them with their enquiries, no matter how insignificant it might seem, to contact the police on these numbers..."

Having seen enough, Suleiman asked Naveed to play both videos. He watches in silence as a procession of black shapes walk in front of a seated couple. It was gruesome. Yet strangely made worse, because the viewer never actually sees the knife enter the body. The executioners stand in front of their victims, with their backs to the camera. Their elbow moves. Or the arm comes up and

disappears from view. But each time they move on, the victim is in a worse state. Suleiman laughs out loud,
"As Lord Anwar would say 'Splendid'.
Then he watches as five seated people had their throats cut. This time everything is facing the camera. The first three have their throats cut. They squeal. Knives are passed. Two more throats are slashed. They gurgle and bubble. Then they are motionless. The camera stays alive for a short while. He nodded his satisfaction.

"Let's not release these yet. Let the infidels dwell on the murders. Let them debate. Let them wonder who did it. Copy-cat or not. I have found that a victim's imagination is often more gruesome than any reality. Let the Englishman imagine the scene. We will educate him at a later date."

"Alhamdulillah," Naveed agreed.

73.

Tom Canning suddenly addressed the room.
"Look at breaking news on Sky."
Everyone stopped what they were doing. They switched to TV networks and there was the scene outside the apartment block in Finsbury Park. While they were glued to their screens, Tom touched the icon for Bernie Durani in the Technical Section in the basement.

"Hi Tom. What's up?"

"You had better get a monitor into the Controller's Meeting right away."

"Can't interrupt that."

"Believe me they will want to see this. Tune it into *Sky News* and get it there pronto. Blame me if you are nervous."

"Wow. Just seen it. OK. Will do."

Faisal walked across to Tom's station.

"What do you think? Could this be why our boys have gone?"

"It doesn't make sense. All they need is a good alibi and we would have a problem trying to pin anything on them. Why disappear? It attracts our attention."

"I agree. Phew. Curiouser and curiouser." He wandered across to talk to David.

By the time Jo strode into the section everyone was discussing the implications of the breaking news item.

"I see you have seen the news." She exclaimed, "We have thirty minutes to come up with an explanation or understanding or even an idea about what this is all about. Is it why our guys have absconded? But then, why those in Brixton? Why Brixton first? Can we find any patterns and connections, anything at all?"

She went across to thank Tom for authorising the techies interrupting their meeting. Then disappeared into her space to give everyone room to be creative.

74.

Tariq and Waheed watched Ibrahim line up the bolt holes for the penultimate van conversion. Then they helped manipulate the large jack system into the back of the vehicle. It was the first time they had got close to the delivery system and they were impressed by its weight. Ibrahim explained that it must be able to hold the roof at an angle while the rockets blast off, so it had to be strong.

Meanwhile in the armoury, Salman and Amir were being put through their paces with the Walther PPK pistols. As these weapons only carry seven rounds per clip, they were the least versatile in their arsenal. Salman emptied the whole clip into the dummy, removing its head completely. This both impressed and irritated Imran. Now he had to find another head.

Amir on the other hand had never fired a weapon before and dropped the gun when it went off. By the end of the third clip he was hitting the trunk of the mannequin repeatedly.

"Always shoot at the belt buckle. You are sure to hit something vital to sustain life," was Imran's mantra for the less experienced gunmen.

Then he fitted them up with a shoulder holster each, to get used to being armed all the time.

Meanwhile, Shami and Sahid were carrying all the bench seats, seatbelts and nonessential fittings into the smaller cellar. They needed the space in the 'stables' to house the converted vans. Although Naveed could not envisage using the beds that Jasmine and Darren had occupied, he did not remove them, but stacked all the superfluous fixtures and fittings in the four corners of that cell.

Whenever Sahid tried to talk to Shami about what had happened in the flat, his older brother shrugged it off. Sahid was feeling irritable and could not sleep. He could not voice his discomfort. He was suffering from withdrawal symptoms. No-one would give him sympathy for that. In fact, he had become afraid of his brother and these other killers. He was sure he was the only coward in the group. He became terrified that they discovered his ineffectiveness. He wondered if they would kill him as easily as they had dispatched the drug dealers. They had been his suppliers for several months. They were his friends. At least he understood them. He did not understand his brother. He had no human feelings.

As the Shah brothers cleared the area in the stables, Hussain filled the space. He was starting up and running each converted van. He wanted to make sure their batteries did not go flat. Then he re-parked them tightly together, to make room for the last two. They did not want any spy satellite or police helicopter to discover an unexplained large number of strange looking vehicles parked up in the forecourt of the manor house.

75.

The Controller's second meeting did not last much longer than the first. As soon as they were seated, he told them that two women and three men had been killed. They were all in their late teens or early twenties. They had all been charged with minor drug offences in the past. They had been mules or soft drug dealers in the area for the past two years. Furthermore, the flat where they were killed was being investigated as a hotspot for drug dealing. Even though was under observation, no police were there when the attack took place.

Then he described the scene. He told them they had been arranged on a line of chairs. They had been gagged and tied to the chairs. The gags were removed just before the execution. He suggested that it intensify the horror aspect of the whole thing for the viewers. Then their throats had been cut. There was no sexual interference with the victims during the executions. Nor were they mutilated in any way, apart from their throats being cut. Both these latter activities were more in keeping with executions between rival gangs.

Therefore, the Controller concluded, they were unique in London crime experience. Maybe they were Islamic State copy-cat murders, but there was no evidence to support this either way. He suspected that it was an ISIS inspired execution. He also expected it to be followed up with something worse. That, the Controller concluded, is what the Counter Terrorist Unit thinks.

Jo reported that despite all her department's contacts, which were extensive, no one could offer a reasonable explanation of why it had occurred. The 'Finsbury Park Massacre' was what the media was calling it. But even they had heard nothing from their network of informers. The best guess was that they had angered a rival gang of drug dealers. They had exacted their revenge as a copy-cat crime of Islamic State videos executing Western hostages. Furthermore, no one could actually link these atrocious murders to the disappearance of the Syrian veterans. The only question that kept coming up was why did it happen on the night they disappeared in Finsbury Park. Which led her to another question. Did something happen in Brixton the night Tariq and Khalid disappeared? We, she reminded them, are still looking for Jasmine and Darren. Were they butchered, she wondered, but remain as yet undiscovered.

Ray Mingdon, the Section Head for Internet Cryptanalysis reported that there had been an explosion in the levels of 'chatter' over the social media and mobile phone messaging. However, he reported that most of it was speculative and nothing sustained. His software programmes had identified several suspect messages from Brixton and Finsbury Park at the time of the disappearances. But they might have been changing SIM cards so were very difficult to connect them. It also meant that there was no chain of contact to identify and follow.

After listening to everyone, The Controller decided that something unprecedented was happening. The tagged Syrian veterans would not have decided to free themselves spontaneously, so it was organised from the outside. As four of them had gone in four days, he recommended involving the police to monitor the others more closely because, he felt, that there would probably be others.

Then in an unprecedented move, he declared that all weekend leave was cancelled forthwith. Everyone inside MI5 was to stay on station. They were to use every contact they had. They were to report anything they felt might be relevant.

He was also informing the Home Secretary to raise the status of alert to red. In other words, an imminent terrorist attack was expected. But no source had yet been identified.

76.

The crew of 'Crescent Moon' rose before sunrise. They went down for their ablutions before going to the small front cabin, set aside for prayer. Then they went through the regular checks that had become their daily routine.

Abdulaziz ran the pumps to clear the bilges. Next he checked on levels of oil in the engine and the charge in all batteries. There were two heavy duty batteries for the engines as well as four leisure ones for everyday life aboard the vessel.

Abdulrahman checked the security cameras. Several people had wandered past the yacht that night, but no one had shown any undue interest. He relaxed a little. Yesterday's visit by the black man had spooked him. He felt as though they were being watched. He was determined to check these cameras every time they had been away from the vessel. Let alone first thing every morning.

After breakfast of nashta – scrambled eggs – and thick slices of bread washed down by lassi, they were ready for the day. Again they had evolved their usual routines. Aziz cleaned through the upper deck rooms. While Rahman was downstairs, dusting the spotless mirrors and TV screens. He vacuumed the upholstery throughout. He could ignore carpets in the less frequently used cabins. There were covered in a tight fitting plastic. This meant that he only vacuumed exposed carpets. He ran though his lordship's master cabin and the corridor leading to their shared cabin aft.

At about nine they received a call from the Hampstead house to say that Lord Anwar was on his way earlier than expected. Rahman checked the fridges. He ticked off all items on their check list. They needed to do a quick shop. Rahman collected two shopping bags. Then he raided the money jar in the cupboard in the galley. He tapped his pockets for the shopping list. It was the fridge contents list. He knew he had to buy all the food stuff not crossed off that list, because it was not in the fridge. It meant that there was no variety in the menu. But it cut out trying to decide what His Lordship might like. Now everyone knew what they could have. He left the vessel en route to the supermarket.

Jackie was on early watch. She saw him leave the boat. As Mervin was in the galley she called down that one of them was going out. Mervin came up on deck and saw Rahman reach the end of Jetty 31.

"Let's see where he goes," he decided.
"Just a minute…" Jackie interjected.
But her colleague did not wait. He vaulted off the deck. Then strode down the jetty. She saw their subject wandering past the end of Jetty 32 as Mervin reached the junction. She watched him fall in behind the quarry.

Five minutes later she saw Abdulaziz leave the boat. She swore under her breath. This was a golden opportunity to bug the boat. But Mervin, her backup had gone. She knew she should wait for him but could not miss this chance to find out what these guys were up to.

Jackie swung down the stairs to the lower galley. She grabbed her small pink backpack. No self-respecting spy would be seen dead carrying a pink bag. Good cover, or so she thought.

She rushed into Mervin's cabin. She pulled the equipment case from under his bunk. Then quickly selected three camera devices disguised as fire detectors. They could also detect fires but could broadcast a picture for up to a kilometre. She put these carefully into her rucksack. Then added six microphone units that looked like screw heads. She was out of 'Dreamland' less than ten minutes after Aziz had left the jetty.

77.

Abdulaziz returned to the boat. He had been to the office to register their intended voyage to the Channel Islands. Then he went round all the lower deck cabins to close the portholes. He felt that the boat had been aired enough. After that, he went to the locker and took out the charts.

Although he had done this journey a number of times, he never left things to chance. There were ten or more generations of seafarers in his bloodstream. This might not the Indian Ocean but he still needed to focus on the voyage. He wanted to familiarise himself with the hazards. He reviewed all ports of call if bad weather closed in. Aziz reviewed the havens for a boat in distress with repair facilities. Lastly, he checked the London Meteorological Office website, to get the latest weather forecast for the English Channel as a whole, over the following six hours.

Abdulrahman returned and stowed the shopping in the galley. He restocked the fridge and freezer. He put champagne in the chill bins along with some white wine. He opened a bottle of red. This was stowed securely in the rack. Thus ensuring that it would be at room temperature and would have 'aired' by the time of serving.

He felt rather than heard the twin MTU 2435 16V 2000 M93 engines throb into life then idle for a while. Then he was making the galley ship-shape. Making sure nothing could slide off the unit tops.

Aziz opened the throttle slightly. The vessel began its slow manoeuvre to the embarkation slope. It was easier for Lord Anwar to transfer from terra firm to a life on the ocean waves.

Abdulrahman knew there was plenty of time. He wanted to satisfy that niggling feeling in the back of his mind. After all, they had both been off the vessel at the same time so it was logical to check the monitors.

Even though he knew something had happened, he was shocked to see Jackie. He watched her exchange two smoke alarm fittings. He memorised the half a dozen tiny devices she put round the lower decks. He watched her freeze. She looked up. Then she scampered from room to room. She finally disappeared into the end luxurious guest cabin. He continued to watch as Aziz wandered through. He even went into the cabin where she hid, closing all the lower deck portholes.

Rahman played it again to get bearings as to where she had put her bugs. Then he went to the toolbox and chose a heavy-duty adjustable spanner. He did not have a plan per se. He was consumed with a feeling of cold fury. Someone had invaded their space. They tried to bug their boat. He was well aware that they were very close to completing the plan. It had taken over two years to evolve and grow their plan. For both these reasons he knew he had to stop her right now.

As the yacht moved majestically towards the landing stage, Rahman made his way to the guest cabin. He knew the layout. There were just two closets to hide in. As the bed

177

was solid, there was no room there. She had to be in the closet.

He opened the cabin door. He knew she would be listening. He went straight to the mirrored closet door. He grasped the handle and yanked the sliding door along its casters. It rattled urgently. Empty.

He grabbed the handle on the second one. As the door rattled along its rail, Jackie launched herself through the gap. Abdulrahman was already bringing the spanner upwards. It connected under her chin with a jaw-breaking crash. She staggered backwards. Her head bounced off the glass. As she stumbled forward, Rahman lifted the adjustable above his head. He brought it down across the back of her head with all his strength. She crashed to the floor like a felled oak.

Rahman felt for a pulse. Nothing. She was seeping blood from her mouth and nose. He tossed the spanner beside her. Then returned to the toolbox in the Flybridge. Glancing round, he could see that they were nearing the pick-up point. It meant that he did not have much time. He grabbed a Stanley Knife and trotted back to the cabin. He went round the edges of the room, slicing though the protective plastic carpet guard. Despite the odd shaped plastic sheet he was able to roll her in the thick plastic, tucking in the odd shaped ends to make sure her bodily fluids remained inside her plastic blanket.

Next, he needed a waterproof zipped container. Something that he could hide her in. But also something that could be discarded over the side. He went to the lower deck store. Here he found a spare green water-proof deck-lounger cover. Rahman took it to the spare cabin. He rolled the plastic bundle containing his victim and the spanner into the cover. He zipped it up. Before he left the room, he found her holdall in the wardrobe.

Rahman ran round the ship, replacing fixtures she had removed. He placed hers in the bag. It took him longer than expected to locate all the screw head microphones she had planted. But once he found two, he knew what to look for. He put these in her pink bag. Then he put her holdall in the green bag with her.

The boat had stopped. He locked the cabin door, then rushed upstairs to help with his lordship's embarkation.

78.

Mervin searched the boat again. This time more slowly. He checked all surfaces where a note might be, then behind furniture, where it might have fluttered. He could not find any evidence of where Jackie might have gone.

If she had popped out to the shops, surely she would have left him a note. He looked at the equipment. Then he discovered three camera fire alarm fitting had gone. This led him to do a stock take of the other spying fixtures. He discovered eight of the imitation screw-head listening devices had also been taken. He went back into the galley and switched on the receiver. There was a faint signal but he could get no visuals and only static on the audio equipment. He tried their two-way communicator. It was good for two hundred metres. Hers was on but she wasn't answering. There were no more excuses. He had to report her disappearance to Thames House.

Faisal was furious that protocol had been ignored. They should not have split up in the first place. Mervin should not have gone off on his own, leaving her alone. But for her to take off on her own without informing her partner where she was going and for how long was against all conventions on surveillance procedure. Even a novice could have pointed out that this precise problem could have been avoided had they both been together.

They finally agreed that she must have gone aboard the 'Crescent Moon'. This was supported by the fact that the equipment was taken. It was logical to assume that she had gone aboard to bug the vessel. This action in isolation, was ill-advised at the best of times. However, it was certainly not to be done on a 'light' surveillance assignment. This was a step, way beyond their original brief.

Finally, Faisal calmed down enough for them to consider their next move. He instructed Mervin to observe the 'Crescent Moon'. But under no circumstances was he to attempt a rescue until he had back up. As Faisal pointed out, at the moment, they had one field Officer missing. They did not want two. Then Faisal said he was going to discuss the situation with Jo and get back to him within the half hour.

Mervin went up on deck and looked to the left. The moorings were empty. He rushed back down to the cabin and called Faisal. He complained that he hadn't even left his seat yet. Then Mervin reported that the vessel had disappeared while he had been below decks. Faisal told him to try to find out where the boat had gone; meanwhile he was getting a helicopter to join the search for the missing agent himself.

79.

Once they left harbour, his lordship retired to the master cabin. He took his official attaché case of notes. It contained a rough copy of his speech. But first, he wanted to read through the relevant notes, in preparation for his appearance before the Committee on Climate Change. It was meeting at 09:15 the following day. He also had an important meeting with a French wind turbine manufacturer in the Channel Isles. He could maximize his time by sailing instead of flying to the meeting, because he found it much easier to work on the yacht.

Once clear of coastal traffic, Abdulrahman showed Aziz the on-board recordings. The skipper was stunned as he put it on 'fast forward'. It made the whole event rather bizarre, like a 1920s silent film gone mad. As soon as it finished, Abdulaziz went back to the main bridge and transferred control to the aft cockpit with direct access to the flybridge.

Next, he collected all the audio and video discs. Then returned to the cockpit and opened the fuse box. He extracted the security camera's fuse. Then popped it into the shower heater slot. Rahman ran down to the first shower unit and switched on the shower. The fuse blew. Aziz slid the blown fuse back into the security camera slot. Then put clean discs into the recorder. Before going below, he checked the sonar screen. Satisfied that they were sailing in an open sea, they went down together.

Aziz assessed the situation. He nodded. Then put all the disc material into the zipped bundle with the body and rucksack. They staggered with the bundle out of the guest cabin. They moved as silently as possible past his lordship's cabin, up onto the rear deck. Aziz was pleased that they had a fixed, solid canopy, which screened their efforts. They scanned round to make sure that they were not near another vessel then together heaved the bundle up onto the side of the boat before toppling it into the sea.

It all but disappeared under the turbulence of the rear screws. Then bobbed bolt upright like a green sea monster dancing serenely in the wake of the ship. Rahman gripped Aziz's shoulder.

"We have to go back and …."
"No. It's heavy. It'll sink."

As they watched the giant bobbing batholith shrank with distance but was still visible a mile away.

"All the evidence is there," Rahman fretted. "If it's found we're dead."
"Yes," agreed Aziz. "But if it isn't found we're in the clear."

Aziz turned his attention to the cockpit. He concentrated on maintaining the vessel's course. It was then that Rahman spotted the helicopter. He knew instinctively that it was looking for them. He wondered if it was the police or British security.

Then he began to fret about their having seen the green bag bobbing in the waves.

80.

Twenty-five minutes after reporting the missing intelligence officer to his Section Head, Faisal was heading south. He was aboard an Airbus Helicopter EC135 T2 Powered by twin 452 kW Turbomeca Arrius 2B2 engines. The pilot, Angus McClusky, was supremely confident that they would find the yacht in the middle of The Channel. Faisal less so. He adjusted his headset and spoke into the microphone attachment that almost touched his lips.

"Hi Mervin. Any news yet?"
"Hello Faisal. Yes, they are on course for Jersey in the Channel Isles."
"Jersey in the Channel Isles," Faisal shouted to Angus. The chopper veered to the right and Faisal felt slightly nauseous. He touched the microphone. "OK. We are in pursuit. Try Jackie's communicator again and keep me informed of any little thing."
"I tried her communicator again but it is dead," Mervin said. "Not any kind of signal now."
"OK. I'll let you know when we have made contact."

Soon they were flying high above the busy sea lanes of the Channel. Faisal was amazed at just how many sea-going vessels of all sizes, scored white 'V' shapes though the green-grey sea below. He was wondering how they were ever going to see Crescent Moon among so many. It really felt like they were looking for a needle in a haystack. Or more accurately, a tiny white arrow on the green velvet baize covered in a chaotic pattern of white arrows.

"There they are!" Angus shouted triumphantly. Faisal jumped.
"Where?" Faisal scanned the sea below. "Can you get nearer?"

The chopper swooped down towards the sea. Faisal's stomach swooped with the craft and he tried not to think about it. Then he saw the unmistakable lines of the vessel they were looking for. It was slicing through the water with the splendour of a young stallion in full gallop across the American Prairies. There was something both majestic yet predatory about the boat below.

"Sierra-Whisky niner-niner two, calling Crescent Moon," Angus recited into his mic. "Can you read me?" He repeated his message twice more. Finally, static echoes over the headsets. Faisal heard the reply.
"This is Crescent Moon. What is the problem?"
"There is a police vessel in pursuit. Kindly allow them to escort you back to Brighton Marina."
"This is Lord Kabir Anwar of Leyton. What appears to be the problem?"
"Good afternoon Your Lordship. I am Angus McClusky of the South East Counter Terrorism Unit. We are in pursuit of an escaped terrorist and believe he may be aboard your vessel. So…"

"This is nonsensical. How could anyone be aboard my vessel? My crew…."

"Be that as it may, Your Lordship. The police patrol boat will be alongside shortly. Kindly heave to and allow them to board."

"This is not the last you have heard of this."

"Again, may I apologise for any inconvenience this may have caused you, My Lord. Kindly heave to and allow boarding."

Faisal watched as the bow wave in front of the 'Crescent Moon' grew smaller. He nudged Angus's arm. Below them the police launch was making headway towards the motor launch.

81.

The Holyhead Marine 15m Patrol Boat was tied up by the Marine Reception at the head of West Pier. No sooner had Mervin stepped aboard then the waters beneath boiled.

"Sergeant Mark Taylor." The red face smiled. "Better come below for your life jacket. Be a bit dryer down there too."

Right on cue, the sea sprayed them as the boat leaned confidently into the water to starboard and sliced nonchalantly into the oncoming waves, making for the open salt water.

Mervin put on a dark blue police waterproof all-in-one and a fluorescent orange life jacket. Then he was briefed on the fact that the helicopter was in pursuit. Mark pointed out that the suspect vessel could speed up to 25 knots, whereas the police launch with its twin Caterpillar C18 (533kW) engines could cruise at 33 knots. Mervin, used to land speeds, felt that the differences were small. But the police officer seemed confident that they would overhaul the suspect vessel shortly.

He was left alone in the salon. There was a big Mess table in the centre of the room surrounded by chairs and three or four bunk beds round the edges. Everything had been screwed to the deck.

Mervin became aware that they were hitting the waves with a rapid repetition which was jarring his backbone. So much so, that he decided to join the crew in the Upper Steering Position. It was precarious getting into the covered shelter of the upper deck. It was exhilarating once ensconced behind the windshield of the thundering cockpit. There was a sort of devil-may-care attitude amongst the crew. They were unperturbed that they were crashing through an alien environment that could swallow them up without a trace at any second. They spoke in quiet confident tones. Like himself in the office at Thames House. It was remarkable what some servicemen come to regard as normal.

"The chopper has spotted the suspect vessel," the sergeant informed Mervin. "Not long now."

"We have a visual." Captain Nicholas Trent had binoculars glued to his face. "They are slowing."

With that the helmsman pulled the throttle lever down slightly and the roaring engine relaxed a little.

82.

Abdulrahman went to get Lord Anwar as soon as the police helicopter made contact. Abdulaziz waited until his employer arrived. He was aware that as the seconds passed they were putting more distance between themselves and the bobbing body bag. He had never seen His Lordship so angry as when he came off the radio. The police officer had sounded very respectful as far as Abdulaziz was concerned. But Lord Anwar was livid.

"They are hunting for an escaped terrorist." Anwar was incredulous.

"Terrorist?" asked Aziz.

"What has it got to do with us?" The Peer queried.

If his lordship was not so absorbed in his own thoughts he might have noticed that Abdulrahman appeared agitated.

"OK." He decided, "We must slow down and let the police catch up."

Aziz reduced speed… a little. Then he saw the patrol boat cutting a beeline straight towards them. He cut speed further.

"Bravo-Oscar-November to Crescent Moon. Heave to and prepare for boarding, please."
"Wallah!" exclaimed the peer. "It's like something out of *Pirates of the Caribbean*. If it wasn't so ridiculous it would be funny."
"Shall we stop in this sea?" Aziz sounded unsure.
"They want to come aboard. What is the best way?" his lordship asked.
"I will slow to three or four knots, then I can still steer. Rahman can throw a net over the side to allow them grip if they fall."
"Do it. I'll wait in the salon."

Rahman reached out his arm to assist the first policeman. Then another policeman boarded their boat. He recognised the black electrician, who had tried to gain access the previous day. He tried to hide his recognition.

They went into the galley and spoke briefly to Lord Anwar. He beckoned Rahman into the luxurious upper salon. He asked his crewman to show them every room and every cubby hole in the boat.

Less than fifteen minutes later they returned to the upper deck. They asked if *Crescent Moon* would accompany them back to harbour. The Captain of the Boarding Party explained that the boat would be quarantined. Once there, it would be forensic examined. The small flotilla turned and headed back to the West Sussex coast.

83.

"We will have to think of returning to land shortly." Angus spoke quietly.

"I think we have done all we can," Faisal reluctantly agreed.

They had been circling the vessels as they came together.

"Sierra-Whisky niner-niner two, calling Bravo-Oscar-November. Come in please."

"Bravo-Oscar-November here. We have boarded, but nothing's turned up. We'll escort the vessel back to the marina. Will await instruction there."

"Wilco. Out." Angus turned the chopper landward and at the same time gained altitude. "Where to?"

"Can you put me down at Brighton Race Course?"

"No problem." And the chopper continued to gain height.

Faisal called Thames House. Jo instructed him to remain in Brighton with Mervin. She said that all weekend leave was cancelled until this issue was resolved. She was arranging for him to be picked up by special branch at the hospital. They would be taking the crew off *Crescent Moon* in for questioning once it returned to harbour.

Twenty minutes later, the chopper touched down just long enough for him to alight. Then with a casual wave of the hand Angus roared off into the night sky. The downdraft angrily agitating his clothes and hair as it left, like a huffy wife not willing to explain why she was in a mood. When he turned round, there was the silhouette of a man beside him. He squinted against the car headlights. A stocky man in a black leather jacket put out his hand.

"Faisal Khan?" he asked unnecessarily.

"Yes."

"Hi. I'm Inspector John Maddox from Special Branch." He looked like a character out of the *Life on Mars* TV programme. Real life retro! "We have procured an interrogation room in Brighton Police Station. Come this way."

They walked over to a silver Jaguar XF Saloon. There were two men sitting in the front. Faisal and Maddox climbed into the rear. With its 3.0 litre 275 Turbocharged Diesel S engine they flew south on Freshfield Road. They screeched right at the traffic lights to join Edward Street. Then a sharp right in front of *The Jury's Out* public house into John Street. They screeched to a halt. On the right was a large lacklustre five-storey block of flats that turned out to be Brighton Police Station.

Maddox led Faisal in the main entrance and said,
"The guys will be picking up the crew members and bringing them here. Hungry?"

84.

Tom Canning sat at his station collating information from Brighton. He kept Jo Pullen up-to-date as the situation emerged. At the same time, he had one eye on the news about the 'Finsbury Park Massacre'. All speculation seemed to focus on rival drugs' gangs. Then at the latest police briefing they tried to reassure the public not to be worried. Inter-gang conflicts tended to target other gang members. Invariably they killed each other while honest law-abiding citizens could go about their daily business happy in the knowledge that they would be safe.

Tom felt uneasy about this. He had seen confidential police photographs of the crime scene. To him it had all the hallmarks of a jihadist execution.

Then his mobile rang.
"Hello big boy."
"Emily." He was genuinely surprised. "Wow. Didn't expect you to get back so fast."
"We don't hang about at GCHQ."
"OK. Have you got some news for me?"
"Yes. We were able to separate the conversations."
"What do you mean?"
"When the device was switched on it began recording then relaying all the telephone conversations taking place in Britain at that time."

"How can you separate them?"

"Thank God for computers. It was just a question of identifying those that started just after the device was switched on. Simples."

"You make it sound simple. Can you tell me what it said?"

"Not over a public phone line. I could come for the weekend…"

He felt excitement course through his body.

"Great. Great idea. Look I'm busy here. Don't know when I can get away."

"That's OK," she reassured him. "We've a lot on. I'd be late anyway."

"OK. Text me when you are leaving, and I'll meet you at the usual place as soon as I can."

"Looking forward to it."

"So am I." And he meant it. He wondered what he would learn from the recording.

85.

Abdulaziz and Abdulrahman were separated on arrival at Brighton Police Station. Faisal and Maddox sat in the observation room overlooking both interrogation rooms. Faisal thought they looked identical. Both had a desk and four chairs, in pairs facing each other. On the table was a clock and a recorder.

As they watched, each suspect was settled by a uniformed police officer. Each sat facing the door. They were asked if they wanted a drink. Both declined but sat nervously perched on the edges their seats. The police officers stood with their backs to the door. Arms folded, unsmiling, in front of the prisoners.

"We can't leave them too long," Maddox said,
"I'm sure his lordship will employ an expensive lawyer to bail them out very soon."
He strode to the door, opened it then hesitated,
"I would invite you in, but if you are still on surveillance…"
Faisal nodded. Maddox shrugged. He led the other three police officers out of the room.

Looking through the mirror was like looking at a huge TV screen. Faisal watched as the inspector entered the first room and started proceedings. The sound came from a speaker immediately below the glass. It was slightly distorted. Also whenever anyone moved a piece of paper or their clothes, crispy noises interfered with the clarity of sound.

Maddox introduced himself to Abdulaziz. He pointed out that he was not under arrest but helping the police with their enquiries.
"Right Abdulaziz," Maddox got down to business, "What we want to know is, did you see anyone aboard your yacht?"
"We see no body."

"Some terrorists have escaped from house arrest, and we want to know if you have seen anyone."

"I do not know about anyone with house arrest. I do not know anyone escape."

"Did you see a woman on your yacht?"

"Many woman on many ships in Brighton. In Yemen no women on a ship. It is man's work."

"No. Not on other craft. Any woman on your boat?"

"Sometimes Lord Anwar bring family on the ship..."

"Not Lord Anwar's family. Another woman yesterday?"

"No. I not see."

Shortly afterwards, Maddox moved to the other interrogation room and started to question Abdulrahman. But the answers were more or less identical to those of Abdulaziz. Faisal felt frustrated. He would have liked to have done the questioning himself, but protocol dictated that he had to leave it to his hosts. Maddox was getting nowhere fast. These guys needed to be left alone with their thoughts overnight then maybe there would be glints of light in their answers.

As if he had read Faisal's mind, the inspector told Abdulrahman that he was going to be put in a cell for the night and asked questions the following day. He indicated that the uniformed officer should take the prisoner away. Then he returned to Aziz.

"Now you have had time to think... is there anything you want to say to me?"

"No, Your Honour."

"I am an inspector, not a judge. Call me Inspector."

"OK Inspector."

"You did not see a woman enter your boat this morning?"

"No Inspector. I went shopping."

"You went shopping. Did she get aboard while you were shopping?"

"No... I don't know... I did not see..."

There was a sharp knock at the door and a uniformed policeman put his head round the door. Before he could say anything, a larger than life, stout figure, clutching a giant document case, exploded past him.

"Ha!" He boomed into the room. "Dear Inspector. Are you questioning my client before I have had a chance to talk to him? Umm? Did you read him his rights?"

"I read him his rights."

"Did you offer a solicitor?"

"Yes I did. I ..."

"No matter. I am here now. I want to speak to my client. Alone, but not in this room." And he tapped the two-way mirror just in front of Faisal's nose. "In a room with more privacy, please."

86.

Tom left the office just as soon as he could after receiving Emily's text. He set off along the Embankment. This time she had managed to get a space in the window.

"Like old times," she said cheerfully. They were squeezed between two large groups of people. Tom found it difficult to hear what she was saying.

"Want another?" he mouthed, pointing at her half empty glass. She nodded happily. Then lifted it to her lips. She drained the glass and handed it to him. He took it. He pushed his way through the hordes of revellers standing by the bar.

Finally he was seen. He ordered a *Peroni* and medium white wine. The barmaid asked which wine. He shook his head. She recited a number of names. He could not hear her very well. He shrugged so she poured one of her choice. It made him feel inadequate. He should know what she liked to drink. Yet they met so infrequently these days. He had an excuse if she complained.

When he returned to the table, Emily smiled at him sweetly. He passed her the drink and they touched glasses. They mouthed, "Cheers!" and took a sip. He placed his glass on one table; she put hers on the other. He felt as though they were in a physical bubble of sound. It was cascading over them constantly, like an unrelenting white-water stream.

"Did you bring the recording?" He had to ask twice.

197

She nodded. Then fumbled in her bag. She passed him the memory stick. He took an earpiece on a long white wire from his pocket and plugged it into the memory stick. He quaffed a mouthful of Italian lager and pressed 'Play'. He could hear the voices quite plainly, despite the bar noise. He listened again.

"How do you stop the British killing Moslems?"

"They…Can hear what you say."

"Don't worry…This jams listening devices. It's safe to talk."

"Are you sure?"

"The camera is pointing in your room. I'm in the doorway. They can not see me. Look busy."

There was a pause…

"You know Christian terrorist attacked for many many years. The IRA bombed London and Birmingham…"

"Brighton…"

"Yes, attacking the British government. But it didn't scare them."

"Stiff upper lip."

"Exactly. London Underground attack didn't strike terror in their hearts."

"Business as usual…"

"Precisely. So, what would stop them?"

"Islamic State killing all disbelievers."

"The attacks on their cities do not stop them. So what would stop the UK from killing Moslems… forever."

"They must follow the words of Allah."

"Al-hum-dull-Allah! In the end. But what is the first step…"

(silence)

He took the earpiece out and wrapped the wire round his left hand before slipping it and the memory stick into his inside pocket. He spoke to Emily.

"Did you listen to it?"

"No." She hesitated then added, "My supervisor told me I was not cleared for this level of departmental co-operation."

"You were always a stickler for the rules. OK. I respect that."

"But?"

"But it doesn't tell us very much. I need to have the whole thing transcribed. I need to go back to my boss and get permission…"

"Who's a stickler now?"

"OK. You win…" He glanced at his watch. "We could just make the next train to Haywards Heath… if we hurry…"

87.

Faisal found the interviews very frustrating. He was not happy when Maddox mentioned Jackie. Now they would know what it was about. Then, if the investigators decided to publish pictures of the escapees; no females would feature.   Again, this would allow them to build up a defence.

It was like showing your cards in the first round. He felt exasperated by the whole situation. He wondered if it had been a female Special Branch Office missing, would Maddox have tried harder. Despite his misgivings, the Intelligence Officer shook Maddox by the hand. They might need him again. For him to air his grievances now, would not change the outcome. It would only be about blowing off steam for his ego. So Faisal held his counsel.

He walked out of the station and turned left. It was getting dark. He reached the end of John Street. Then crossed Edward Street and into *The Jury's Out*. As a Moslem, he knew alcohol was taboo. His father would be mortified. But as a British agent he had developed a taste for Real Ale. So, after the frustrations of the day, he had a pint of *Bombardier*.

Halfway down the glass he felt strong enough to check his messages. There were three from Jo. He listened to them before asking the barman to call him a cab. He would answer them on the street while he waited for his transport.

An hour later he was sitting with Mervin in the salon aboard 'Dreamland'. They both felt despondent. Mervin went to the galley cupboard and took out a 25-year-old bottle of Chivas Regal. He poured a generous helping into two whiskey glasses. Amber highlights flickered on the wall as he brought them to the table.

"I blame meself you know," began Mervin. "If I hadn't 'ave followed Abdulrahman round *Asda* she'd still be alive today."

"We don't know she's dead."

"Use your common sense man," Mervin quaffed his drink. "There's no way she's just gone out for a walk and got lost. Not after all this time."

"OK. Have it your own way," Faisal conceded. "But where's her body?"

"They dumped it overboard. Before we got there. I'm ninety-nine percent certain. Overboard."

"They were pretty smart about it. We were hovering above them soon after they set off. If they dumped her, surely someone's seen something."

"We found no evidence when we went aboard."

"Forensics is going through her with a fine tooth comb. If she was aboard, they'll find some traces." Then Faisal had another thought. "Could she swim?"

"What?" Mervin would not be consoled. "She would've been picked up by now. And we'd 'ave heard by now. No."

"All the time forensics have the yacht in quarantine the Islamists are making alternative arrangements." Faisal voiced his frustrations.

"Can we get the boat back to them soon? Pity we blew our cover." Mervin asked.

"They are good, but they can't perform miracles."

88.

Lord Anwar arrived at the Palace of Westminster for the Committee on Climate Change meeting at 09:15 in Room 15. However, he did not go there immediately, but visited The Right Honourable Hajaz Akram QC.

"Hajaz." The elder statesmen shook hands sedately.
"Kabir, my dear friend. How are you this splendid morning?"
"Fine. Fine. And you?"
"I am well. Thought it would be better if we met here. The walls do not have ears in here... or at least they shouldn't."
"How did it go last night?"
"No problem." He waved his hand to a chair. "One of my more experienced barristers soon had them out. Any more questions will be dealt with through my office. I don't think you will be bothered again."
"What's behind this? Do you know?"
"It's a bit unusual. There is a veil of secrecy thrown over it at the moment, but I've put out some feelers through the Home Office. We should know soon enough."
"Thank you. If there is anything I can do for you?"
"No. Not at all. It is a pleasure to help an old friend."

They shook hands affectionately and Lord Leyton hurried to Room15, hoping the debate had not started without him.

89.

After Sun Rise Prayer everyone congregated in the dining room for breakfast. As usual, Naveed Nazir delegated jobs for that day.

Hussain and Ibrahim were to cut the roof off the last white van to be converted.

Tarik and Waheed were to install four tubes on the second to last van's roof.

Khalid and Nazir were to put the jack fitting in the same van.

Shami and Sahid were to get themselves armed. Once Imran had armed them he was to begin activating the warheads for the rockets. The Shah brothers were then to use the big screen monitor in the sitting room to visit their target on *Google Earth* to get a feel for its layout and surroundings.

Everybody took their dishes to the kitchen after the meal. Hussain put them in the industrial sized dishwasher. Then he cleaned the dining room and wiped down the kitchen surfaces. Meanwhile, Ibrahim organised the lunchtime mezze. He prepared a number of small dishes on the central table: soft white cheese, melon, nuts, various salads and dips, such as tabbouleh, hummus, mutabbal and pickles. These were arranged in the middle of the long table where everyone would come for lunch. Lastly he put out English white sliced bread, because it would not go hard before the meal. He threw a large linen sheet over the food to protect it until lunchtime.

90.

Everyone clustered round Tom's work station just inside the operations room. He slotted the memory stick into his CPU and played the recording over the speakers. Everyone exchanged glances when it had finished.

"It was just getting interesting…"

"Is that all?"

"Where is the rest of it?"

Jo raised a hand for silence, then spoke, "OK. We should have got the whole lot debugged but we did not want to share information before we knew what it was."

"Well…" Began David, "we don't have all the information we need because of that... erm… policy."

"You are right," Jo agreed. "But, let's be positive. What have we got here? Play it again, Tom."

Again the room remained silent except for the accented voices ringing out clearly.

"For one thing… that isn't Lord Anwar," Observed Tom.

"So who the devil is it?" Asked Malcolm.

"What accent is that?" Tom asked. "Arabic? Turkish?"

"Not Turkish," decided David. "I would say he was a Gulf Arab."

"A Gulf Arab?" exclaimed Malcolm. "How the devil did he get into see Tariq when the politician was there?"

"He must have arrived with the peer," Jo said. "Anyone know how he got in?"

"I'll look back at the papers and newsreels. If we have a visual of his arrival or departure from the Siddiqi household..." David volunteered.

"We need the information from the rest of the tape," Tom reasoned. "It looks like they are planning an attack which they believe would put the brakes on our country's Foreign Policy."

"And the Arab sounded pretty confident that it would work. So what the blazes did he say next?"

"OK." Jo decided. "Get the rest unscrambled as soon as... if not quicker."

91.

Suleiman arrived at Gayhurst Manor shortly after 10:30. He was taken on a guided tour of the five finished vans. They looked authentic, with their 'Crescent Moon Sanitation Company' stencils firmly attached. He was also pleased to see that in the *CMSC* logo - each 'C' was a sickle moon - and contact information clearly listed on the side of the vehicles.

"What happens if anyone rings the number?" Suleiman suddenly asked.

"Well..." Naveed laughed. "It doesn't actually exist. The number stimulates a ring-tone spool. It will go on for ever.

Also, the website looks good, but none of the links work. So if anyone tries to make contact they will believe that the company is incompetent."

"That would be awful," laughed the Saudi. "Just imagine."

"Come. Let us see Imran Iqbal at work."

They went down to the cellar. There was a circle of light on the work bench, like a stage set for a *Hammer House of Horror* movie. Imran wore white shapeless protective clothing. He looked like a spaceman. When drawing near, they could see he had one of the conical warheads out of its lead-lined case. He was connecting wires inside the cone itself. When he saw them approach, he put the cone into the case and closed it carefully. Then he removed his cumbersome floppy helmet. It reminded Suleiman of a bee-keeper he knew as a child.

"Salam-o-alaikum," greeted the Saudi.

"Alaykumu salam," the Syrian replied.

"How is it going?"

"Good. I should have all the warheads ready this evening."

"Are they bunker-busters?" Suleiman wanted to know.

"Yes. They are the latest technology. They will go in deep before they explode. Wonderful technological development. Bunker-buster bombs used to be so heavy, to literally 'bust' in... but these... they are amazing."

"And the rockets?"

"Another day. Two at the most."

"Alhamdulillah," Suleiman and Naveed said together.

"We are almost ready to strike," Suleiman said gleefully.

Then they went to the sitting room. They played both discs again, before deciding to release the 'Finsbury Park Massacre' first. The Saudi felt that it was still fresh in the British psyche. It would also undermine all that the authorities had said about the event.

As they planned to publicise it on *YouTube*, it would be easy for the authorities to trace where this 'film' had been uploaded. They had to do it from a public place. Suleiman decided to drop Naveed at Wolverton Station where he could catch a train into Milton Keynes. He could use any internet café in the middle of MK and up-load the 'movie' online. Afterwards, he could catch the bus back to Gayhurst. Suleiman had to get back to London to pick up the peer so could not do the return journey.

Naveed went up to his bedroom. Fifteen minutes later he reappeared cleanly shaven, in a crisp dark blue business suit. Suleiman was impressed. He could remember how difficult it had been for him to shave off his beard when he had first come to the UK. All his life it had been drummed into him that Mohammed the Prophet had not shaved. Furthermore, it was imperative that a true follower of Mohammed must not shave off his facial hair. But Suleiman knew it was important to blend in. Men in big beards, especially with Middle Eastern appearance would

207

be watched very closely by the general public, let alone the police. So it was vital they assume these disguises. But he felt for the sacrifice Naveed had just made.

"Allah will bless you in heaven for the sacrifices you make in his name on Earth."

"Allah-be-praised."

92.

"Jo!" Tom called across the office. "The Controller's on the phone for you."

She gave him the thumbs-up and made her way back to her own space. The Controller was terse, asking her down to his office, immediately. This rarely happened, but she still collected a coffee on the way. Then knocked at the heavy oak door. She heard his voice and entered. But he was not alone.

"This is Lord Bolden, Parliamentary Under-Secretary of State for Internal Security. Let me introduce Josephine Pullen, Project Manager of Monitoring Terrorists under house arrest."

"I am pleased to meet you Ms Pullen." The civil servant was civil. "I have heard a lot about you. There are openings for ambitious project managers like yourself. I trust that you are thinking of making your career in MI5."

"Thank you very much. Likewise, it is a pleasure to meet you."

"Good. Now let me come straight to the point. We want you to leave Lord Anwar alone."

"But he was present when a recording was made in one the suspect's houses."

"A recording. What recording?"

"When he visited Mrs. Siddiqi," She began, "Someone in his entourage approached Tariq. He's tagged. And has been instructed not to speak to anyone… "

"Where is the recording?"

"On my computer."

"I want you to delete it."

"Delete it?"

"Can you do it from here?"

"Yes," interrupted The Controller. "It is possible for Ms Pullen's computer to be accessed from here." Jo had not realised that. She tried to recall anything private she had done on her computer recently.

"OK. Delete it now. That is an order." Lord Bolden looked uncompromising.

Jo walked to The Controller's desk. He moved aside. She sat in his chair. She could see her icons on the screen. She accessed her database. Found the file, hesitated, then deleted it.

"Is it permanently deleted?" Lord Bolden demanded.

"It will be when we break the connection to Ms Pullen's computer," The Controller stated.

"Do it," he instructed.

With a heavy heart she returned to her chair. The Controller broke the link.

"Now Ms Pullen, recall your surveillance officers from the marina. I have already called off Brighton Special Branch and the yacht will be returned to Lord Leyton this afternoon. And..." He waggled a finger at the crest-fallen Section Head. "Let this be the last we hear about it."

"Yes sir." She felt like a schoolgirl in the headmistress's office. "I will recall them as soon as I return to my office."

"You'd better go then, hadn't you?" Lord Bolden dismissed her.

93.

Ibrahim Caan was teaching Nazir Bashirn and Khalid Ahmad how to fit the jack into the rear of the second to last van. Then they would go on to do the last one by themselves. At the same time, Tariq and Waheed began to fit the firing tubes onto its roof. Now they had the experience, these jobs were becoming easier. There was now a time pressure on them to finish these conversions so the actual attack could be brought forward.

Once more, Naveed started the five finished vans to warm the engines and charge the batteries. He also checked the air pressures in the tyres and oil level in the sumps. Lastly he checked the liquid levels in the windscreen washers. They wanted to make sure no van was dripping oil or had a slow puncture on the final journey.

Naveed parked them more tightly together. There was just enough room for the driver to clamber in at the rear door. He had to make room for the last two conversions. Once that was done, they had to clear up the 'garage'. It would be needed in the timed launch of the vans on the final day. When that time arrived, the vehicles could be spread out, to allow easy access for the armourer to set up the rockets. He would also be needed to attach the warheads. Then the drivers would need access to prime their satellite navigations systems. Space would be crucial on the day.

94.

"Check out *Sky News*." Tom called across the room.

Everyone stopped what they were doing. They congregated round his work station rather than look on their own. It was as if they needed some moral support for what they knew would be another hammer blow. And shock it was, even to these experienced intelligence officers. The video of the 'Finsbury Park Massacre' was briefly viewed. But it had been sanitised to allow viewing by the general public.

Tom split the screen. He tapped into YouTube and sure enough they soon had the unedited version. Together, they watched the gruesome story unfold. Then the website was shut down. Tom searched and found a new one.

"It has been programmed to regenerate itself," Tom informed them.

Just then Jo returned from her meeting with The Controller and Permanent Secretary. She was pleased not to be centre stage. Even she was shocked by the gory images relayed on the screen. The whole thing crashed again.

"At last," Tom exclaimed. "*Google* are taking their responsibilities seriously."

"What do you mean?" David Jones asked.

"Whoever sent this to *YouTube*," Tom informed his audience, "Had it reproduce itself so whenever anyone closed it down, the British authorities I think this time, it regenerates itself. Only the service provider has the wherewithal to actually change that. Interesting. American pressure I am sure."

Jo beckoned for Tom to follow her. Everyone was absolutely riveted to the breaking news item and did not notice them disappear across to her space. She was highly conspiratorial and he was feeling a little uneasy with the situation.

"Did you make a copy of the conversation in the Siddiqi home?" She asked suddenly. "Because I was ordered to destroy my copy on my computer. Which, of course, I did."

"Do you want me to destroy my copy?"

"I don't know you have another copy, do I? I forgot that I have already authorised you to pass it on to your contact in GCHQ. And of course you are unaware of my being bollocked for having a copy." He nodded imperceptibly.

"But of course, it is imperative that only you and I know about this copy. If you happened to have one. And... and the fact that we are going to get it unscrambled." He nodded uncertainly.

"No one," she drew her face very close to his, "I repeat no one must know we are following this up." She smelt of peppermint. "I feel that it is essential information for our investigation. I refuse to allow departmental politics to interfere with justice. Is that clear?"

"Perfectly ma'am." He wondered if she had just brushed her teeth.

"Good." She sat on her swivel seat and waved him away. Once Tom had left the office she texted Faisal to report in. Three minutes later her phone rang.

"Ma'am. Faisal here. What can I do for you?"

"You are coming home."

"Great. Who will replace me here with Mervin?"

"No one."

"What?"

"No one. Tell Mervin to pack his bags. Help him pack Jackie's stuff. Remember, to keep it clean for her family. Understand?"

"Of course. But..."

"Then vacate the boat. We are pulling out."

"Ma'am. I don't believe..."

"Enough. That's an order. The surveillance has been called off. Bring everything with you." She hung up before he could question her further. She was developing a migraine headache right across her lower forehead.

Two hours later Tom met Emily at *The Prince of Wales*. She had travelled from Haywards Heath to meet him because she wanted to see '*Phantom of the Opera*' again. While they were sipping their drinks he repeated what had been said. She was very unhappy about continuing with the arrangement. She felt that the chain of command was important in government departments. She was not happy that his manager was going behind the back of her superior.

It was only the urgency to leave in time to catch the show that made her relent, but her proviso was that she would not be privy to the contents of the communication.

Later, Tom was to regret agreeing to her condition.

95.

On Sunday morning there was no dawn. The heavy rain gradually became more visible. Naveed wondered if this would be better on the day of the attack. He had seen everybody at early prayer and again at the dawn prayer. After breakfast he wanted to delegate out the jobs. Time was becoming paramount.

Imran informed him he had finished the warheads. Next he was going on to prime the rockets.

Salman Pervez and Amir Mahmood were told to put the rocket cradles into each van. They were to be arranged in pairs. Two pairs on each side.

Tariq and Waheed were to weld on the four tubes to the last van roof. As soon as they finished, Khalid and Nazir were to attach the roof to the jack mechanism in that van.

Ibrahim Caan and Hussain Ahmed were to go over the Land Cruiser V8, fill up with petrol then to be on standby for the final pick-up.

Shami and Sahid had to clean and set up three more bedrooms, making sure they had two beds, enough blankets, soap and a couple of towels.

Once everyone had gone, Naveed went to the storeroom. He unwrapped the new number plates. They were arranged in pairs. An oblong one for the front and a square one for the rear. They were brought into the dining room. While Hussain and Ibrahim cleared up the breakfast things and prepared a mezze for lunch. He set out the number plates, proof of ownership documents and insurance papers in sets, along the dark oak table at the rear of the room.

96.

Although Sunday is the Christian day of rest, Moslems accept it as The Weekend. However, they do not have the same attitude to certain events not being allowed on the Holy Day. Although nowadays very few Christians observe these traditional restrictions. It is especially true since shops were allowed to open on Sunday. Suleiman had planned to find out what was happening to Crescent Moon. Then he was summoned by His Lordship.

One of the congregation from the Birmingham mosque had just been killed in Syria. Lord Kabir wanted to advise the Imam how to deal with the British media. He always advised the Imams to emphasise the family's sadness at their loss. But then to stress their bewilderment that one of their children could ever think of fighting in a Jihad. Finally they should emphatically deny that the young man was following the true Moslem teaching. After all Islam is the religion of peace and brotherhood for mankind.

Suleiman had expected there to be more reaction to the problems relating to the boat. He had been unnerved by the death of the British agent. Then the subsequent impounding of the vessel and the questioning of the crew. All could lead the authorises to him.

Suddenly the British Secret Service were interested in his host and it would not take them long to find him. All his instincts of self-preservation were screaming at him to act right away. As soon as he had got the message from Lord Leyton that he was to drive him to Birmingham, he rang the three contacts, asking them to meet him at the mosque.

The journey seemed eternal. There was the usual slow mass movement of vehicles on the M1 and the M6. Then they had the bumper to bumper crawl through Birmingham itself. They finally arrived on Middleway. As usual, he ignored the main entrance and drove to the large car park at the rear. There were not many city mosques with an adequate car park. But Birmingham was the exception.

As soon as his lordship went up the steps to the Imam's office, Suleiman disappeared. He went into the kitchen for a cup of sweetened lassi and a honey cake. Ikram and Adnan were waiting for him. This time he paid for their snacks before going into the room at the back.

97.

Faisal was sitting at his work station going through the evidence again. He had the Statement from Lord Anwar, which said nothing. Then there were the transcripts of the interviews with Abdulaziz and Abdulrahman. At least John Maddox from Brighton Special Branch had managed to get them to him before being warned off. But they were not really that helpful. Then he thought about the recording of someone plotting something with Tariq. Whoever it was then seemed to have disappeared off the face of the earth.

"Who was in the car with Lord Anwar?" he asked himself. He searched for newspaper photographs of him on that date. Then it hit him. The chauffeur. Of course! How stupid! He was always with the peer.

He searched the database for details of Lord Leyton's staff. Sure enough he came across his work permit. Suleiman was indeed a Gulf Arab, he came from Saudi Arabia. He had entered Britain two years before and almost immediately joined the staff of Kabir Anwar as a chauffeur.

Faisal downloaded the permit, his photograph and the references. It was impossible to contact the Saudi Embassy on Sunday. That was his first job on Monday. He would not hold his breath, because from past experience, those at the Saudi Embassy could be extremely obstructive. Alternatively, they would bend over backwards if it was in their interest. But terrorism was their soft spot. They were totally paranoid about it. Ever since 9/11 revealed Saudi involvement, they could deny its existence, no longer. They had lived in a perpetual state of denial up to that point. Even blaming Infidel Alcohol brewers of bombing attacks rather than admit they had a terrorist problem. After that they had to join the '*War on Terror*' declared by George double-yeh Bush.

He printed off hard copies of the documents. While they were printing he went across to the stationary cupboard and got out a buff file. He punched holes in the printouts and laced them into the file. He went back and printed copies of the interviews which he also put in the file. He rearranged the papers chronologically and wrote "Suleiman Al Dossari" across the front. He placed the folder squarely in the middle of his desk. At last, he had a named suspect.

Next, he went into the DVLA database and found the numbers of all his lordship's cars. Again he downloaded all the bumf and printed it off. This was put in his new file. When he had identified the Bentley as the car most driven by Suleiman, he took the number across to Tom's desk and said,

"Are you or are you not the 'Digital Intelligence Tactical Solutions Developer' of this section."

"Yes," Tom answered suspiciously, "Though I'm not sure why you have given me my full job title like that. You're after something. I know you."

"Because I want to see if you can develop a solution for me."

"Oh! I see. What's the problem?"

"Can we trace the movements of this vehicle through the motorway traffic cameras or town centre security camera or those in the multi-storey car parks?"

"You've been watching too much *Spooks*. You've been in MI5 long enough to know that TV isn't real life."

"Blah... de-blah... de-blah... blah. Come on Mr Digital Solutions Developer, work your magic spells."

"As you asked so nicely, I will see if I can link into their systems."

"Is it possible?"

"I only saw the second series of *Spooks* so I don't know. Now piss off and leave me alone with my machines. At least they don't ask inane questions."

98.

Hussain stopped in the slow lane of Belgrave Middleway. According to the sat nav they had reached their destination. They could see the mosque off to the left-hand side behind a chained-up gate in an unbroken fence. Ibrahim pointed ahead to a side road. They pulled back into the traffic then first left onto Frank Street. Hussain took the next left on Highgate Street and left again into Highgate Close. This brought them into the Birmingham Central Mosque car park. They could see Lord Leyton's Bentley, so pulled alongside. No sooner had the engine noise died then Suleiman himself came over to greet them. They shook hands then touched cheeks. The Saudi lead them into the rear room where four men waited.

After introductions, Ibrahim collected all their electronic equipment. He extracted the batteries, placing them in his leather multi-pocketed backpack. While he was doing that, Hussain got Ikram and Adnan to carry their baggage out to the van.

As soon as they had gone, Ibrahim talked to Bilal Zaidi and Nadeem Naeem about picking up their tagged comrades-at-arms. Once they had a decided their schedule, they too carried their bags to the vehicle.

They stacked the bags in the luggage space behind the last row of seating. Ibrahim and Bilal joined Hussain on the front bench. Nadeem joined Ikram and Adnan in the back. Hussain started the engine and Suleiman waved them off. As soon as the van left the car park, he went inside to wait for Lord Anwar to conclude his business.

99.

"He's in Birmingham now," Tom reported to Faisal. "I can show you."

Fifteen minutes later Faisal, Malcolm and Davy Jones were being driven at top speed across Vauxhall Bridge. They veered onto Nine Elms Lane en route to the London Heliport Tours Ltd., in Battersea.

Meanwhile, Tom was speaking to Angus McClusky. They arranged the London pick up, in his Eurocopter EC135. Their destination was Birmingham International Airport. Lastly he contacted Special Branch at Birmingham Central Police Station. He arranged for his colleagues to be met at the airport. Then to be taken to see all the local tagged returnees from the Syrian conflict.

Less than an hour later, they landed at Birmingham Airport. A marked police vehicle was waiting at the parking apron where they landed.

"Hi. I'm Faisal Khan with Thames House." Flashing his warrant card. "This is Malcolm Brainchild and that's David Jones. All from the same section."

"Nice to meet you. I'm Inspector Michael Zimmerman and this is Sergeant Gladstone Abrahams." They shook hands while he continued, "He'll stay with you today. He'll drive you anywhere you wish to go. But first we'll go to Birmingham Central for a briefing with the police. They are, as we speak, checking all tagged suspects' homes. OK?" Everyone nodded. He smiled and moved towards the Ford Tourneo People Carrier. "Let's roll."

As they got into the high visibility police vehicle Faisal smiled and turned to Zimmerman.

"Special Branch in Brighton had a three-litre Jaguar..."

The Inspector answered in a broad brummie accent, "They're just flash gits down south."

That broke the ice between the two groups. They felt more relaxed together, in the rear of the people carrier. Faisal was well aware that sometimes there was bitter rivalry between regional and capital police forces. He often found resentment towards him simply because he was from The Smoke.

100.

Bilal directed Hussain north on Upper Highgate Street then left onto Leopold Street. They stopped at a block of flats on the left. Hussain pulled into one of the designated parking bays. Bilal led Ibrahim up three flights of stairs. They went along a corridor but stopped outside a newly-painted bright blue door.

Bilal rang twice, put his key into the slot and opened the door. They went into the dimly lit hallway. Bashir Ibrahim emerged. He was short, clad in a long grey thobe. He was sporting a huge bush of a beard to show his devotion.

Ibrahim put a finger to his lips and Bashir nodded. Bilal moved past his cousin into the bedroom. Ibrahim took the cutters and wire clips from his backpack. It did not take long to clip the wire then snip though the tag. Bilal emerged with two small suitcases. Again Ibrahim collected Bashir's phone and electronic watch. He removed the batteries and slipped them into pockets on the outside of the backpack.

Without a backward glance, they left the apartment and made their way to the Land Cruiser. Bilal and Bashir clambered into the back, greeting their friends, while Nadeem got into the front with Ibrahim to direct Hussain to the last pick-up point.

Mohammed Malik was a totally different sort of detainee. He had short hair, was clean shaven and wore stylish western clothes. After Ibrahim cut him free he went into the bedroom to collect his CD and DVD collections. Ibrahim took his iPhone and iPad, removed the batteries and packed them into the backpack with the others. Mohammed lingered in the doorway of his flat looking round nostalgically before joining the others.

They pulled away and turned right, then right again, until they came to the road they had been in. In fact, as the van slowed for the traffic lights at the end of the road, a police vehicle zoomed past them, blue lights flashing and siren whining. It jumped the lights and turned into Mohammed's street.

"Looks like we just made it."

Mohammed did not realise how near the truth he was. However, it created laughter in the comfortable comradery in the dark of the vehicle, as they bonded in the zealous mission ahead.

101.

Gladstone dropped them on Steelhouse Lane at the doors of the rather grand Edwardian façade. Surprisingly it was the Central Police Station, opposite the Birmingham

Children's hospital. The Inspector led them up to the second floor and into a small office. He had commandeered two desks, four assorted hard-backed chairs and a water dispenser. He could do nothing about the banks of over-stuffed filing cabinets that either supported or were supporting the outside wall.

"We cleared this out for you," Zimmerman explained, "Use it as your base. DS Abrahams will be in shortly. He'll show you the canteen and toilets in the basement. I'll return as soon as we have reports from all the mobile units knocking on doors as we speak. It shouldn't be long now."

Inspector Zimmerman left them alone. Fifteen minutes later, the detective sergeant took them on a tour of the station, stopping in the basement café. They each bought carry-out drinks and snacks to take to the office upstairs.

Sipping lukewarm coffee and tea from thin polystyrene cups and sharing a packet of *Rich Tea* biscuits, Gladstone regaled them with stories of his West Indian family growing up in Birmingham. He broadened his accent to make it more authentic. Faisal related his experiences as a member of a huge Pakistani family growing up in London. Then the inspector burst into the room.

"Right. Grab your things. We're on the move."

They filed out of the office, clattered downstairs and strode out of the front door. Then they stood waiting for Gladstone to collect the transport.

Five minutes later they were heading south along The Great Charles Street Queensway. When they entered the mosque car park, Suleiman was washing the windows of the Bentley. Faisal studied him carefully as they drew near. Gone was the black beard to be replaced with a large black moustache, but clean-shaven chin. He was wearing a black, single breasted suit and black peaked hat, the epitome of a chauffeur. Faisal climbed out of the police van and walked up behind him.

"Suleiman Al Dossari?" As he turned, Faisal read fear in his eyes.
"My name is Faisal Khan and I am with British Security Service."
"Yes?" The Saudi turned back to clean the car.
"I heard your conversation with Tariq Siddiqi." Faisal saw his hand freeze on the windshield. "What have you got to say about that?"
The Saudi turned and looked him in the eyes.
"Who did I talk to? What are you…"
"Suleiman!" Lord Anwar was standing on the top step of the mosque. "Suleiman. Do not talk to this man. Can I see your ID?"
Faisal took out his ID card.

"Suleiman." His lordship was commanding. "Copy these details for me."

The chauffeur took the warrant card into the limousine and copied Faisal's name and number on to a piece of paper.

"You will be hearing from my solicitor very soon." Lord Anwar waved for the return of Faisal's warrant card then stepped deliberately into the back of the Bentley. The Intelligence Officer had been summarily dismissed. Suleiman climbed into the front and they drove off as sedately as royalty.

Twenty minutes later, Faisal and team had visited the home of Mohammed Malik and Bashir Ibrahim. They confirmed what the police had just discovered. Their respective tags had been removed in exactly the same way as those in London.

Then they were driven back to the Central Police Station where Inspector Zimmerman promised that the patrols would check on the other tagged suspects randomly throughout the night. It was agreed that there was nothing for them to do. So the Task Force from London were returned to Birmingham Airport, on their way back to the capital.

102.

Monday morning dawned with a milky light, as a river mist sent a mystical chill across the Buckinghamshire countryside. Eighteen residents of Gayhurst Manor jogged through this ghostly scene, like phantoms from another world. They had been up for over two hours starting with the first prayer. Naveed wanted them to feel the adrenaline buzz of physical exercise on their penultimate day.

Breakfast was a noisy affair. The six new members were being quizzed by the ones who were already there. They were particularly interested in the public reaction to the so-called 'Finsbury Park Massacre'. Also Tariq had fought beside Mohammad and Bashir. They had a lot of catching up to do. Ibrahim realised that they would be moving out soon, so was using up his stock. He boiled twenty-four eggs as well as making a giant omelette.

When everyone had finished, Naveed called for attention. He welcomed the new arrivals. They were to spend the morning with Imran. They were to practise with their firearms. Although three had experience with side arms, these were different. Then Imran would help them become familiar with the firing mechanism of the launchers. They had to raise the launch tubes to the correct angle. They had to type in the correct co-ordinates for the target area. There was a lot to learn. Now the pressure was on. The police seizure of Crescent Moon had put the cat among the pigeons. Suleiman had insisted on bringing the attack forward to the following day. Everything needed to be finished today.

Tariq and Waheed were to finish spraying the last van. The Shah brothers had to put the new number plates on all the vehicles. Then they needed to make sure each vehicle had the correct legal documents. If the police stopped the vehicle, they needed proof linking the new number plates with the supposed owner. Then they should be able to go on with their journey. At least it should minimise any delay.

Salman and Pervez, along with Khalid and Nazir, were to bring the missiles from the cellar and to put them in their slings in the rear of each assault vehicle, four per vehicle. There was a new urgency. Seeing the missiles being loaded up brought butterflies to many a stomach. The banter died down and everyone got on with their chores, quietly.

There was no more 'what if...' or 'supposing...' it was now a reality.

103.

Tom and Emily parted at the entrance to Charing Cross tube station. Before disappearing into the bowels of the earth, she promised to prioritise the debugging of his recording and he promised to speak to her every day. Then he bought an 'i' newspaper from the vendor at the station.

It was a chilly Monday morning and commuters were swarming along Villiars Street towards him. He moved along the station side, struggling against the tide of shuttling humanity. Then he passed the Embankment Tube Station and crossed the road. It was quieter here. He stopped and stared at the River Thames. He could smell its heavy water in the morning air. He remembered that smell when he was a child, on a canal holiday. He stood for a moment and glanced at the paper.

Sanitised pictures of the Finsbury Park Massacre appeared on the front pages of all the nationals. The 'i' was trying to be different as usual. That was what Tom felt. But it still questioned the spread of IS influence in Britain. He wondered how Faisal really felt when he saw his own ethnic and religious group instigating such barbaric atrocities. But on top of that they did it in the name Allah. They did it in the name of God.

Tom's mother was from a staunch Protestant Northern Irish family. He knew that at least two of his cousins were involved in killing Catholics. This was just the same really. But he wondered, could he have worked against them. Faisal was one of the best field officers they had in the department. He was like a terrier with a bone. He really wanted to prevent another attack. And it was his energy and foresight that had brought them this far. But these were his people. They did it in the name of his God.

Religion was responsible for so many deaths and outrages throughout history. All in the name of God. Yet, most religions aspire to be about love. How far from the truth, this was in reality. The Jews, Christians and Moslems were all responsible for different genocides, massacres and torture throughout the last two thousand years of European History. But who would take them to task? With a heavy heart he continued his journey to Thames House.

No sooner was he in the office than Faisal approached him holding his warrant card inside a specimen bag.

"Tom. You're our 'Digital Intelligence Tactic…'"

"I know, I know, I know…" Tom interrupted abruptly. "So what do you want now?"

"Suleiman Al Dossari, Lord Anwar's chauffeur, handled my warrant card. I've dusted it down for fingerprints. I can see three or four almost complete ones. Can we see if they are in the terrorist databank?"

"Yes we can. But your elementary methods will not produce clear enough prints for us to use. We'll have to send the card to forensics for a definitive print that will stand being digitised and compared with the database."

"How soon can we do this?"

"Is this the same Lord Anwar we have been told to leave alone?"

"The same."

"So why should I put my neck on the block?"

"Because I know that he is behind these disappearances. Here is an actual chance of getting real evidence... real proof that will make The Controller realise Jo is right."

"Cover for me. I'll get this down there right now."

Faisal sat at Tom's station as he went to see if forensics could do a quick job for him.

It was not just the fingerprints. He needed them digitised as well.

104.

Towards lunchtime, as the groups finished their morning tasks, Naveed called a meeting. It was for a communal lesson. Ibrahim was going to demonstrate how to operate the jack device for lifting the roof. In order to do this properly he needed one of the completed vans. He drove it under the clock tower. He hid it below the entrance arch, so any passing satellite or a police helicopter would not be attracted to the strange structure.

The Islamic fighters were already divided into pairs. After the initial demonstration, each pair took it in turns. First they had to imagine stopping the vehicle with the front pointing at the target. To facilitate this each vehicle had a dome-compass attached to the dashboard. Under each compass were the coordinates so the driver could line the van up. This was in order for the rockets to launch in the precise direction. It was imperative. There was only vertical change that could be made to the trajectory of the missile through raising the roof.

Once the van was 'aimed' at the target, the driver would get into the back and enter the second set of numbers. These were the target co-ordinates. They needed to be entered into the on-board computer attached to the jack. This would elevate the roof to the correct angle to hit the target. If the jack failed to open automatically, there were two cogs. These could be rotated thus raising it manually. By reading the dial, they could open the roof as accurately as the automatic method. Except for the effort and stress caused by having to improvise when on a mission. Each pair practiced opening the roof, both automatically and manually.

At the same time as the driver was arranging the roof tilt, the co-driver was busy. He was to take the yellow tarpaulin and two road signs out of the rear of the van. Not forgetting to close the rear doors afterwards, so the missiles would not be seen. He must arrange the reflective canvas to screen the rear end of the vehicles. Then he had to place two '*Men at Work*' signs either side of the van. One in front and the other behind, near the vehicle but not on them. Finally he was supposed to remove the protective lids from the front of the roof tubes.

Next both fighters must attend to the rockets. There had to work in tandem for it to work smoothly. The driver armed the warhead by twisting it in a clockwise direction. Then the co-driver must open the rear fittings for all four tubes. Next both men would lift the missiles out of their hammocks, one at a time, and push them into the shafts. When they were safely inside the tube, one man would close the fitting, while the other would clamp it in place. This activity had to be repeated four times. When all the missiles were in their respective tubes, armed and ready to fire, they should stand back. There was only one thing to do. The last act was to take the remote control out of its sleeve in the door. Push the red button and fire the missiles.

In order for them to achieve martyrdom they should stand immediately behind the vehicle. Then they would go directly to heaven and the reward a jihadist receives when he dies for Islam.

Ibrahim supervised each pair through the routine before lunch. Then he returned the van to the stables. Naveed drove the Land Cruiser out onto the street. After lunch, another van was put in the arch under the gate tower. Everyone had to run through the routine once again. As Ibrahim said, practice makes perfect.

While they were engrossed with the second run through, Naveed collected the last DVD. It was showing the execution of Jasmine and Darren. He collected Hussain. They squeezed past the practice in the entrance arch. Then opened one gate wide enough for them both to exit.

Hussain got in behind the wheel of the Land Cruiser. He drove them directly into Milton Keynes. They parked in a multi-storey car park in the town centre. They were careful to chose a different internet café.

Ten minutes later they were on their way back to the car park. But already people all over the world were watching the Jasmine execution tapes.

105.

Tom was the first to see the news flash and called the others over. They crowded round the terminal and he pressed 'replay'.

"Take a still," Jo suddenly spoke from the silent group, "Before Ray Mingdon's lot takes it down."

Tom took a couple of stills of the Mujahid talking directly to the camera. Then another of the whole group before the site crashed.

"Well done Ray," Jo said.
"It will reboot itself," Tom said. Then he showed the stills.

"Isn't that Jasmine Siddiqi?" Jo asked. "I'm sure it looks like her."

"Yes you are right," agreed Faisal.

"So that must be Darren," Jo assumed.

"Bloody hell," Davy Jones said, "They are just kids. They have their whole lives ahead of them. It's so bloodthirsty, so bloody callous."

Then the movie popped up again.

"Here we go," observed Tom, but this time he took an actual copy of the film before it crashed again.

"Give the stills to everyone in the section," Jo instructed. "See if you can recognise any of the perpetrators. I know Computer Intelligence Section has facial recognition software. But sometimes we can do it the old fashioned way. Those bastards in the masks must be her family. Get as many identified as possible." And her high-heels rang angrily all the way to her space.

106.

After Naveed returned to the manor he called everyone together in the sitting room. He explained that they were nearing completion of their tasks and if all went well, they would attack the following day. A ripple of excitement shimmered through the listeners. He told them that it was quite possible for a member of the general public to ask them what they are doing. He said that the British public have been told to be on the look-out for Islamic attacks.

So everyone had to shave all their facial hair off. They must not look like Moslem fundamentalists. But if a member of the public asked them what the rockets were for, he advised them to say they were sewerage torpedoes. They were designed to travel independently along the sewer. They could take photographs and find leaks. The assembled fighters laughed at the argument but realised that they might be questioned by a passer-by.

He then showed them a business card for 'Crescent Moon Sanitation Company'. Each van would have a collection of these cards; some for them for the sanitation officers themselves, but some for an up line manager, if a member of the public wanted to complain to the company. Naveed emphasised that they should politely divert any questioners away from the area and finish the task in hand. Polite but firm was his mantra.

He emphasised that the final preparations were as important as the first. As the paint was touch-dry he asked Tariq and Waheed to put the company transfers on the last two vehicles.

Khalid and Nazir were to attach the plastic sleeves onto the rear right door of every truck. This was to house the remote control.

Salman and Amir were to change the number plates on all the vans and make sure the insurance papers were in the respective glove compartment.

Mohammed and Nadeem were to check that every vehicle had the tarpaulin, road signs, the launch remote and mallet to drive in the metal supports for the screen.

Shami and Sahid had to check the oil level, windscreen washer water level and tyre pressures of all eight vans.

Ikram and Adan had to use *Google Earth* to check their target and become familiar with the area. Then make sure that all the missiles were secure in their net hammocks ready for the journey.

Bashir and Bilal had to report to Imran to practise using their pistols and be fitted for their holsters then to go onto *Google Earth* to get to know the vicinity of their own objective.

Finally, Hussain and Ibrahim were to arrange the vehicles in order of departure. The first three were to be lined up in what had been the maintenance garages, the work benches had been pushed against the rear wall to make room for the vehicles. The other four lined up in the stables. That would give Imran enough room to fit the warheads just before the vehicles left the following morning.

107.

Jo Pullen picked up the office phone. It was The Controller asking, rather tersely, to see her immediately. She had a bad premonition about this call. Despite that nagging feeling, she popped into the canteen and collected a coffee en route to her summons. She was not going to be bullied.

When she knocked at the door it was opened by Ray Mingdon, who was leaving. She could not read the expression on his face. Then she was in front of The Controller's desk. That feeling of doom surfaced again as she saw Lord Bolden, Parliamentary Under-Secretary of State glowering beside him. Both of them sat, symbolically, on the other side of the desk.

"Sit down please Josephine." The Controller opened his palm towards the chair opposite.

"Thank you, sir. Good afternoon Lord Bolden," She greeted her superiors.

"Good afternoon," He whispered. "What part of 'Back off Lord Anwar' did you not understand?"

"I'm sorry?" She looked at The Controller.

"Did you know that Faisal Khan harassed Lord Anwar's driver yesterday?" The Controller asked.

"Sorry sir, this is the first I've heard about it." She wished Faisal had warned her.

"Can't you control the people in your department?" The Lord spat the words at her.

"I did pass on your request that…" She tried to explain.

"It was not a 'request' it was a 'directive'."

"As I said, I did convey your…"

"I am really disappointed in you," Lord Bolden confessed. "I could see you going far in the Service. But... but this blatant disobedience..."

"With all due respect..." Jo interrupted, speaking through clenched teeth.

"I think you should stop there." The Controller saw her anger. "We need time to assimilate what has happened, but... but I am sending you a formal disciplinary letter highlighting your shortcomings in this matter; for instance, your disregard of instructions from a superior officer. Have you got anything to say?"

"No sir. I did not realise that Lord Bolden was a superior officer."

"That is impertinence Pullen," The Controller exploded. "I will not have it in my department. Do you hear?"

"Of course sir." Jo tried to relax. "Sorry sir. I will find out exactly what..."

"That goes without saying... but... take it as read that you are now on probation. I have asked Ray Mingdon, the head of Internet Cryptanalysis to act as your mentor. You will run everything past him before you sanction any actions. And... I mean any action. If anything else untoward emerges, you will be summarily dismissed, without any references. Is that clear?"

"Perfectly."

"Good. Now get back to your section and discipline Mr Khan for his blatantly disobeying your orders."

"Thank you Controller. Good day Lord Bolden."

"Good day," he replied without grace.

108.

Hussain showed the residents how to programme a sat nav. All fourteen of them clambered aboard the Land Cruiser. He ran through the demonstration in the van before they left. He advised them to put the co-ordinates in to the device while the vehicle was stationary. This he explained was for two reasons: firstly, it allows the driver to leave in the correct direction, immediately, but secondly it is against British law to be fiddling with a sat nav or a mobile phone while driving. He made the point that if they were pulled over for fiddling with a sat nav. It could jeopardise the whole mission. They must not endanger the assignment through stupidity.

Then they set off towards Newport Pagnell. Several times his students changed co-ordinates. They got used to the verbal messages and how to respond to them. What caused most confusion was...

"Recalculating. Recalculating."

When they got back to the manor, Hussain took them into the dining room. His last instruction for the day was to advise them to follow the speed limit at all times. They did not want to jeopardise the whole mission because they were picked up by the police for speeding.

"Under no circumstances attract attention. Obey the Highway code at all times. Then you should arrive at the launch site on time and in good condition."

It was time for Maghrib Prayer. There was an air of excitement buzzing through Gayhurst Manor as they adjourned to wash noses, ears, eyes and mouths, then feet and hands, to be clean enough for evening prayer.

109.

Faisal left Jo Pullen's Office suitably chastised. She left him under no illusions about her feelings concerning his transgression in approaching Lord Anwar's driver. It was especially galling so soon after having been warned off. He had tried to explain why he had done it. But she was having none of it. She absolutely refused to look at his new dossier. Then she pointed at the door with the promise of a disciplinary letter in his personnel file within the hour. In fact, she was dismissing him so she could write it.

Faisal went across to Tom.
"Did you hear that?"
"We all heard it. One of the drawbacks of an open plan office. In this office the walls indeed do have ears." They laughed at the paradox.
"I know Suleiman Al Dossari is our man. But I've been warned off." He flopped into a wheeled computer chair

next to Tom. The latter smiled and turned his screen so the recently chastised might see.

"I've got one piece of information you might like," Tom switched user and tapped into the police surveillance cameras. "This was taken outside an internet café in Milton Keynes at about the time the Jasmine's execution movie was put on the net."

"Those two?" He pulled his chair nearer. "Not your typical bearded wonders."

"Yep. Then later, walking through the multi-storey car park… Then… leaving in this van."

"Did you get the number?" Faisal could not keep the excitement from his voice.

"Yep. Finally circling the motorway roundabout for Newport Pagnell."

"Did they go on the motorway?"

"No. They just cut across the roundabout. But…" Tom paused for effect.

"But what?

"My guess is that they live quite near there."

"Man. Can you believe that?"

"You are slipping." Tom observed.

"How do you mean?" Faisal looked bemused.

"Because, you did not ask me about the van ownership."

"OK. OK. Who owns the van?"

"Metropolitan Police."

"A police van?"

"Auctioned off last month. Not registered to anyone else… yet."

Faisal sat for a few seconds then asked, "Can you trace the Bentley now."

"God Almighty, Faisal. When you go down you want to take all of us with you."

But he hacked into a different region police camera system. He looked at the registration number on a yellow Post-it-Note attached to his tower. They watched as a recording showed the Bentley pass under a bridge. Then saw it cruising along a dual carriageway travelling from right to left. After five minutes of tracking, Tom said, "Well, looks like he's been a good boy. Went to the House of Parliament twice and home between times. Not much to write home about there."

"Damn. What about the day before? Can you go back?"

After half an hour, they discovered that he had been on the M1 on several occasions during the past two weeks. Furthermore, he always used the same exit; Junction 14 for Newport Pagnell.

"The same roundabout as the van from the internet cafe," Tom confirmed.

"Can you put out a police alert on the Land Cruiser?" Faisal asked.

"Yep." Tom typed the van's number into the webpage. "Now every mobile police unit in the Home Counties will be on the look-out for that vehicle. Anything else?"

"No. Phar! It is difficult to maintain patience in this game especially when office politics gets screwed up."

Tom laughed then got on with his job, trying to remotely fix a camera located in the home of yet another returnee from the Syrian conflict. But this one was different. He had been fighting for the Kurds against the Islamic State.

The paradox of war! The enigma of Intelligence!

110.

There is about an hour and a half between Maghrib and Isha Prayers. During that time, Naveed showed them their vehicles. They had been placed in order round the two sides of the quad. The first three vans housed inside the garage and the remaining four in the old stables. The eighth van, the Land Cruiser, with its new registration number, was parked in the archway below the clock tower. It was hard against the wooden doors, just in case the British authorities decide to attack.

Naveed told each pair of Mujahedeen to sit in their vehicles.
"Become familiar with its layout. Adjust the seats. Make yourself at home."
Then they had to prime their sat nav for the journey. They were to save the first six-figure grid-reference as 'home'. Then all they had to do was select 'home' before they set off the following day. It would automatically activate the correct destination. That would save stress on the big day.

The second set of co-ordinates was for the target. They had to feed these into the roof-jack computer. It would raise the roof to the correct angle to hit the target effectively.

In the first van, Tariq Siddiqi and his brother, Waheed, were nearest the clock tower on the left, just inside the main gate. Their grid-reference for their destination was 329936, while for the target was 359949.

The second van was manned by Khalid Ahmad and Nazir Bashirn and they were to drive out of the same garage door. Khalid entered 528294 into the sat nav and 535265 into the on-board computer.

In third place were Salman Pervez and Amir Mahmood, who would exit through the last stable door on the left. They entered 261453 as their home address and 219468 as their target.

Then from the first door on the right Mohammed Malik and Nadeem Naeem would follow Salman. They typed 413572 and 391599 respectively.

Fifth, emerging from the same door would be Shami Shah and his younger brother Sahid. They entered 462711 followed by 509741.

The sixth to emerge, would be from the second door on the right driven by Ikram Khan. He would be accompanied by his cousin Adnan Abbas. Their numbers were 086207 followed by 089161.

Lastly, from the third stable door, nearest the house, Bashir Ibrahim and his cousin Bilal Zaidi would sally forth. They were the last arm of the attack. Their new home reference was 702953 while their objective was 651999.

Each of the teams sat in their vehicles to examine the papers. Then they checked the tarpaulins, remote control, road signs, mallet and jack system of their particular vehicle.

They returned to the house for the late night prayer and their last supper together. Everyone was in high spirits. Soon they would meet their fate, in the name of Allah. There was no greater sacrifice a man could make than to give up his life for his God. Thus was the sermon from Imam Imran in an inspiring rally call to the faithful.

They broke bread together for the last time. The moment was charged with emotion for everyone, but especially the younger ones who had not been to Syria or Afghanistan nor fought in Iraq.

After the meal the more experienced fighters regaled their captive audience with colourful accounts of their exploits.

They described beheading foreign captives. They recounted seeing thief's limbs being severed and infidel women raped. Imran talked of shooting scores of blindfolded traitorous prisoners. Shami remembered burning Christian Churches and Jewish Synagogues. They all relished the destruction of Infidel places of worship. Tariq recalled blowing up buildings and witnessing martyrs going to heaven in a blaze of glory. Allah rewarded the ultimate sacrifice of being a martyr for Islam, with a guaranteed seat in paradise.

Several times,
"Ash-hadu an la ilaha ill-Allah," (There is none worthy of being worshiped except for Allah)
Could be heard from the audience. But the most common phrase circulating that gathering was:-
"Allah al Akbar" (Allah is greater)
They were entering the correct state of mind in preparation for the ultimate Islamic sacrifice.

111.

"Faisal. You were right." Tom waved his hand urgently.
"What have you got?" Faisal moved to stand beside his workmate.
"Your instincts were spot on."
"Stop the flannel. What've got."
"The results of your fingerprint samples."
"Suleiman Al Dossari, the Saudi Arabian chauffeur?"

"No. Jābir ibn-Gharsi, from Yemen. A founding member of AQAP. Which is *Al-Qaeda in the Arab Peninsular*. He is wanted by the Americans for several attacks. But especially the one on the American warship in Aden harbour on 12 October 2000. Seventeen American seamen were killed… and 39 injured."

"Wow." Faisal sat down heavily on the spare chair. "This puts a completely different complexion on the whole thing."

"It certainly does."

"Give me a copy and I'll go chat to Jo."

"I've already sent it to your laptop. Not your desk top. This is your baby. Make two copies. One for your file and one for Jo. Let her study it. Then she can focus on it while you talk her through it and… And it gives her something tangible to take to The Controller. If she so decides. Good luck."

Tom watched Faisal scamper to his station to find the file on his personal laptop computer. He downloaded the material and printed it off. He put the print-outs in his buff folder. Then he stood and picked up the folder. Like a soldier on parade, he squared his shoulders, winked at Tom and marched to Jo Pullen's space.

Tom was distracted as his mobile vibrated. He removed it from his pocket and looked at the screen. It was from Emily.

"Emily. Just can't get enough of me…"

"Hi Tom. Just thought that you'd like to know that the transcript of your recording is here."

"Read it to me."

"I can't..."

"What do you mean you can't?" He felt techy towards her.

"It was handed to me in a sealed envelope and I was instructed to pass it to Josephine Pullen, Project Manager for Monitoring Terrorist, in person."

"You're joking?"

"No. They think it is dynamite, and... not for general consumption."

"I gave it to you."

"I know. Not even you have this level of clearance."

"What is it? The bloody Ten Commandments?"

"Look. You involved me. I am just doing my job. Neither you nor I are allowed to see this because it needs a higher security clearance. That would be your boss, Josephine."

"We need this now."

"I'll see you tomorrow. I'm booked on the 11:45 National Express from Cheltenham Spa arriving Victoria Coach Station at 14:20."

"Fine. I'll meet you and bring you straight here. OK?"

"Great." Emily gushed, "Looking forward to seeing you tomorrow. I'll be able to stay over. But must be back in Cheltenham early, in time for work."

"Fantastic," Tom agreed. "Looking forward to seeing you. Bye now."

"Bye darling."

And she hung up. He sat back smiling. She had never called him 'darling' before.

112.

Imran did not attend the predawn prayer. He was kitted out in his CBRN (Chemical, Biological, Radiological, Nuclear) suit. He looked like a deep sea diver. He stood next to the first vehicle. Tariq and Waheed carried four lead-lined flasks from the cellar. These were placed them on the ground, behind their vehicle.

Imran slowly unscrewed the first silver canister. He carefully tipped the dull grey cone into his left gauntlet. Tariq opened the rear door wider. The armourer leant into the van. Then painstakingly screwed the warhead onto the first missile. This action was repeated three more times. Then the first two fighters went in for prayer and breakfast. But there was no such break for the bomb-maker.

Khalid and Nazir brought up their four flasks and placed them reverently behind their vehicle. Khalid held the van door open for the armourer to reach in. Once he had attached the four warheads, they too went in to finish their breakfast. And so it went on until all the missiles were armed and ready to be activated.

In the meantime, Naveed led the predawn prayer. He read from the Quran, the Islamic Holy Book itself. He read Chapter 78 – sūrat l-naba (The Great News) – verses 29 to 34. First he read it in Arabic so that everyone could catch the nuances of the original text. Despite that, he immediately translated into English one verse at a time.

In it Allah promises that all martyrs will go straight to heaven; the land of milk and honey with 72 virgins for each warrior in "fulfilment of their Heart's desires". He emphasised that Allah had revealed this through Mohammed the Prophet, peace be upon him. Furthermore, today they had the opportunity of fulfilling their destiny as true devout Moslems. Then and only then would they live in blissful happiness for the whole of eternity.

While the troops were having breakfast, Ibrahim brought his knapsack from the cellar. He placed all the mobile phones, watches and other electronic devices on the hall table. He laid them in a line across the dark oak, like on a stall in the market. Then he paired up the batteries, as best he could. These were placed beside their devices. But he did not put the batteries into their counterpart. These would be a crucial part of the final act.

113.

The night before, Jo had unofficially sanctioned Faisal's latest scheme. They agreed to act independently of the department. Jo felt that she could not trust her upline manager to act decisively. Also because of the infighting that had erupted between her and the hierarchy. They were dictating to her without listening to anything she said.

Tom felt that their identifying the fingerprints of Jābir ibn-Gharsi, would soon be known. It was imperative for them to stay one step ahead of the management, if they were to take advantage. It was agreed that Malcolm would sign out an unmarked saloon immediately. Thirty minutes later Tom Canning would do likewise for a mobile communication truck.

Jo had a key to 'the company' safe house on Smith Street in Watford. She had acquired it some weeks before, when they were thinking of putting Faisal's contact somewhere safe. Even though the emergency passed she kept the key. She wrote the post code three times. She tore off each one. Malcolm took the first as he went to sign out the first vehicle. Tom took the second and returned to his work space. Faisal took the last one and the key.

Shortly afterwards Faisal left the office. He took his latest file with him. He went straight down to the car pool. Malcolm was waiting for him. He had signed out a black BMW 3 Series Gran Turismo 3.0 litre. They climbed aboard and left Thames House by the staff entrance.

The safe house had a large attached garage that would house both the truck and the car. As soon as Malcolm pulled up in front of the double doors, Faisal scrambled out. He unlocked the door and slid it up into the recess. The BMW pulled over near the wall. Faisal pulled the roller down then unlocked the door into the house.

Upstairs in the living room were all the communications equipment needed for a surveillance operation. Faisal got onto the radio phone and contacted Mervin. He had already been joined by William Fox. They were to continue monitoring activities on the 'Crescent Moon', which had been returned to Brighton Marina. Faisal emphasised that they were only to communicate with Jo Pullen or himself. Mervin was quite happy to comply. He was still angry that Jackie had not materialised.

Two hours later Tom arrived. He stopped outside the garage doors. He had managed to procure a Ford Transit 3.0 litre V6 decorated with the 'Openreach' logo. This they hoped would allow them to blend in anywhere. No one asked an Openreach operative what they were doing. It was sure to be about fibre optics. Faisal rattled the rollers onto their drums. It was a tight fit to squeeze the van in with the car, but they did it. Now all they had to do was survive till daybreak without being discovered by MI5.

At 06:00 the next morning, they wandered down Smith Street and turned right on King Street. They wandered past the Probation Office and came to the High Street.

They found a café open. It advertised a full-English breakfast served all day long.

Faisal did not have bacon or sausage but had extra fried egg and toast. He admitted that he had not slept well. Malcolm boasted that he could sleep anywhere, anytime. They agreed that was an essential skill in their kind of job. Tom was worried about meeting Emily's bus that afternoon. They agreed to cross that bridge when they came to it, but if necessary, Jo could meet Emily.

They returned to the safe house and Faisal rolled open the garage doors. Tom climbed into a Ford Transit. It started first time. Then Malcolm pulled out in the BMW. They waited for Faisal to lock up. It would not go down well at Thames House if an MI5 safe house was burgled because someone forgot to lock the garage doors. Soon they were in the bumper to bumper nightmare that all residents of Watford face every day. They inched their way towards the M25.

The countdown starts...

TEN...

At exactly 06:30 the first 'Crescent Moon Sanitation Company' maintenance van pulled out. It left through of the front gate of Gayhurst Manor, resplendent with its distinctive tubular storage units on top. The Siddiqi brothers were in fine fettle. Perhaps it was because they were first to leave the compound. They was no time to feel nervous or have second thoughts. Also, they were still exhilarated by Naveed's pep talk.

He told them they were going to change history. No more would the infidel state, Britain, kill innocent Moslems. Shortly, sharia law would be imposed on the whole country. When the other European countries saw the benefits they would want to join too. The British society was damaged and needed a moral compass. Sharia law would provide them with a moral backbone again. It is what every good Moslem wanted to hear.

The sat nav helped them negotiate through Birmingham motorway system. Then they motored north, skirting Stoke-on-Trent towards Warrington. They veered west from the M6 onto the M56, then the A494, before swinging north on the A55. They followed the North Wales Expressway as far as 'Valley'. They turned right onto the A5025 heading north again. It was getting on for 11.35. Even though neither of them could understand all the road signs, the sat nav took them unerringly towards Cemaes and their date with fate.

At Tregele they turned left onto a narrow country lane which twisted and turned to the T-junction at Tyddyn Sydney. The van bore left at the next three-way stop and then right past sharp gorse bushes. Twisting right then left to the penultimate right-hand turn marked by an untidy cheese-shaped wedge of earth in the middle of the road. Ignoring the left-hander they drove across the Causeway and the sat nav informed them:

"You have reached your destination… on the left."

Three vehicles were already parked in the car park, opposite the monument. One was near the end where they wanted to be. Tariq reversed the van tight against the concrete wall at the far end of the untidy car park. Waheed looked at the compass and directed the driver to angle the van on target. It meant inching forward at a strange angle. They hit the right number and Tariq drew on the handbrake.

The time was 11.42.

Waheed clambered out of the van, stretched and strolled to the rear. Opening the rear door, he pulled out the yellow tarpaulin. He began to screen off the side and tail end of the truck. Meanwhile, Tariq walked to the front and removed the protective covers from the ends of the tubes. He tossed them into the space between the van and the wall. They would not be needed again. He returned to the cab and tipped the driver's seat forward allowing himself to squeeze behind. He squatted under the controlling mechanism.

Although it was tight, he had practised enough. He confidently checked the numbers on the jack dial. He touched the button. In response, the roof of the vehicle began to yawn open. The four tubes began to point skyward. This was the critical moment. If they were interrupted or stopped now, their part of the mission was a failure. He focussed on the dials. The front part of the roof rose perceptively. The van took on a different profile, more like the vehicles seen on TV in Libya or Afghanistan or Iraq.

Having finished hammering in the supports for the reflective screen, Waheed went back to the truck and dragged out two road signs. One he placed at the front of the vehicle. The other he took to the entrance of the car park. He opened the supporting easel. 'Men at work' it proclaimed. He walked back to the truck. Its roof had opened at an angle of about 50 degrees. He looked round nervously. If anyone should drive in now, the van would look strange with its roof gaping open at the front like that.

With renewed energy he hurried behind the screen and yanked open the retaining clips on the four roof tube flaps. Each circular hatch swung down to expose the gleaming silver barrel into which the missiles had to be loaded. Once all hatches were ready, he opened the rear van door to its fullest extent. The four missiles nestled comfortably in their harnesses in the aluminium frame undisturbed by their journey.

He knew that the Lightweight Multirole Missile was only thirteen kilos. But it was one and a half metres long so could be cumbersome to balance. Especially with its warhead securely in place. That made it top heavy. He knew he should wait for his older brother, but heaved the first one towards him. It was heavy but moved easily. The fin twisted in his hand so he nearly dropped it.

"Tariq. Quickly."
His brother clambered out of the front door and trotted towards him.
"Wallah. What is the matter with you? You should have waited for me."

Together they pulled the silver projectile clear of the cradle. Tariq expertly twisted its warhead to fully activate it. They looked at each other. There was no going back now. Together they lifted the missile into the first tube. It was a tight fit and took their combined strength to slide it home. Waheed shut the hatch and Tariq clamped it home. Then they proceeded with the others.

When they were done, Tariq looked at his watch; 11.58. It was time, he cried,
"Ash-hadu an la ilaha ill-Allah", twice
Then took the remote control from its bracket on the rear door.
Waheed intoned "Allahu Akbar" four times.

They looked at each other and Tariq lifted the remote.

They stood directly behind the van. They were immediately incinerated as the four rockets ignited simultaneously. They did not see the burning trajectory of the four rockets arc majestically into the bright midday sky on their way to Wylfa Nuclear Power Station.

NINE...

At 07:00 the second truck departed the clock tower gate. It was soon on the M1. However, it did not leave at the M6 interchange like its predecessor, but rather continued northwards to Junction 49. Then they went on the A168 towards Hartlepool. Their sat nav steered them between Stockton-On-Tees and Middlesbrough onto the A19 and the Wolviston roundabout. Here they turned right onto the A689, Stockton Road. Traffic was becoming heavier. Nazir looked at his watch yet again.

"Com'on. It is getting late."
"We will be there in time, Inshallah."
The traffic slowed to negotiate a parked delivery vehicle. Then over the bridge at Seaton Carew mainline railway station.
"There are only fifteen minutes left."
"There is time if we keep cool. Inshallah." Khalid tried to sooth his young relation. "Keep cool man."

They reached the coast, with the flat featureless sea gleaming ahead. Khalid swung the van to the right, along The Front, towards Seaton Carew golf links. At the links they kept left and into the large car park on the sea front. Because it was such a blustery day there were few cars. Even the dog walkers had gone home early and the golfers were waiting for a calmer day.

Khalid drew the van as near the southern end of the car park as possible, joining a row of five other cars. With some toing and froing he was able to get the correct angle according to the dashboard compass.

"Get the screen in place." Khalid felt he should keep Nazir focussed.

Then he smiled. The younger man slipped on his shades and ran his fingers through his hair before pushing open the passenger door. He sauntered round the front of the vehicle before reaching up to unscrew the covers. These were tucked into his coat pocket. Then he strolled casually to the rear of the vehicle. He swung open the right hand door and dragged out the yellow tarpaulin. This he threw open on the ground behind the van.

A motorist stopped and looked at him. Nazir began to sweat. He fumbled the reflective yellow material onto the catches near the rear off-side door. Then he paced out three big steps and began hammering a metal rod into the tarmac.   Out of the corner of his eye he watched the motorist turn away to find another place to park.

While this was going on, Khalid squeezed onto the rear seat. Because the glass was blacked out, it was difficult to see the dial. Nervously he pressed the red button. He glanced at his watch.

11:52. Nazir was right, they were cutting it fine.

Meanwhile the younger man placed two 'Men at Work' road signs just outside their tarpaulin. He opened both rear doors of the van and looked at the missiles in their cradles.

"Excuse me." He spun round to see a face peering at him over the tarpaulin. "You can't just come in here and do what you want, you know."

Nazir just froze. He was unable to speak. Unable to move as the other man went on, pointing at into the back of the van.

"They look like torpedoes. What are they? What are you doing here?"

And he began to move along the tarpaulin to gain entrance by the wall.

"They are." Khalid emerged confidently from the front of the vehicle.

"What?" The car park official stopped in his tracks.

"They are investigative torpedoes designed to run along sewer pipes to find damage."

"Oh! Well you still can't come…"

"Look, why don't you ring my office." Handing the wavering official a business card, "And check that we have the correct authority."

"I'll have to ring my office as well…"

"Good idea. Double-check."

"Don't do anything till I get back."

"No. We will wait for your say-so."

Slightly appeased, the official marched off to his booth near the car park entrance.

"It is time."

Khalid glanced at his watch: 11:57. Nazir released the clips and Khalid opened the hatches. Together they pulled out the first missile. Khalid armed the warhead and they slid the first one home. Khalid held the hatch cover while Nazir clamped it in place. They did the second and the third, when they were aware of the attendant shouting from his booth.

"Oiw. You. Stop that!"

"Keep cool." Khalid grabbed the last missile. Nazir armed it and together they pushed it into place. They shut and clamped it as the attendant shuffled across from his box.

"I've warned you already." The car park official tried to enter the enclosure. "Stop that at once. You have no..."

"Ash-hadu an la ilaha ill-Allah,"

Khalid shouted at the top of his voice, stepped round the side of the van and pushed the button. All four rockets ignited and blasted Nazir and the attendant. If they screamed, it was drowned in the roar of the missiles as they shot into the sky, on their way to Hartlepool Nuclear Power Station.

EIGHT...

At precisely 07:20 the third group pulled away from the manor. However, they turned left and headed for Milton Keynes.

Amir had managed to retrieve the watch Faisal had given him from the pile on the table. It had taken him longer to identify the correct battery. He was afraid that Ibrahim would know if he put the battery in, so he waited. When Salman was busy negotiating the country lanes he slipped the battery in place unnoticed. Then he put the watch around his wrist. They had almost reached the M1 junction when he managed to switch the wristwatch tracker on.

Immediately this signal was picked up in the surveillance van that was still in transit to their vantage point under the Newport Pagnell motorway bridge. Tom Canning pulled over and pushed his way into the rear and switched on the tracker. He called Faisal on his mobile communicator.

"Tom? Why did you pull over? Do you need assistance?"
"Your contact has just started transmitting."
"Wallah! Where is he?"
"Looks like they are making for Junction 15. Next one up from where we expected them."
"That still fits in with our premise that they live nearby."
"True. Do you want me to follow?"
"No. I'll follow the tracker on our mobile, but you stay at the bridge. Jo expects to join us there. As Amir knows me, I might be able to make contact before anything catastrophic happens."
"I'll let you know if they change course," Tom volunteered.
"OK. Let's burn some rubber." Faisal gave Malcolm the thumbs up. The Gran Turismo's Twin Power 3.0-litre engine roared into life. It zoomed at over a hundred and twenty miles an hour along the northbound carriageway to intercept the suspect vehicle. Tom blinked as he watched them disappear. Like watching The Enterprise go into warp speed in Star Trek.

Motorway cameras would later record that they followed the same route as the first group as far as Birmingham. But instead of turning north onto the M6 they turned east onto the M46, then joined the M5 south-bound. Salman was becoming aware that Amir was fidgeting more and more.

"Are you nervous?" The Syrian veteran asked.

"No. I am going to be a martyr for Allah."

"Why are you so nervous, if you will give everything for your God?"

"I need to go to the toilet."

"The schedule is tight. It will have to be a short stop."

Soon afterwards the motorway sign for Strensham Service Station loomed up. Salman pulled into the slow lane ready to exit the motorway. The pursuing BMW had tried to keep three vehicles behind them.

"At last," Faisal observed. "We'll play it by ear. Amir might not have much time."

The sanitation van followed the directions to the HGV Park at the back of the complex. Once there, Salman backed between a lorry and a campervan.

"I could do with a pee myself," Salman admitted.

"OK. You go first and I'll stay by the van." Amir sat back and looked far too nonchalant. Salman hesitated. Alarm bells of suspicion were ringing loudly in his ears.
He added, equally relaxed,
"I won't be long."
He walked towards the building, but didn't go in. He waited in the entrance lobby, looking at the reflection of the van in the double doors.

Meanwhile, the BMW pulled into a space at the front of the building with a view of the lorry park.
"Can't see the van," Malcolm complained.
"Look. You stay here. I know Amir. He trusts me."

Faisal eased himself out of the car and moved swiftly round the vehicle holding his portable tracker in front of him. As he neared the van he could see why they could not see it from the other vehicle. It was neatly sandwiched between two much larger vehicles. As he neared the truck Amir emerged from the off-side front seat and stood in the shadow of the lorry.

"Amir," Faisal whispered as he neared.
"Ah! Be quick. He will return soon."
"Where are you going?"
"You will not believe the plan."
"Quickly. Tell me."
"We are going to destroy this country."
"I don't understand. Where were you hiding?"

"In a big house. Big buildings and many vans."

"Many vans like… "

Faisal froze. He felt something very hard pressed above his right ear and someone grabbed the back of his collar. Amir stared wide-eyed focussed on a point behind the intelligence officer's left ear.

"Get into the van now." Salman's voice was quiet but both men heard him plainly. Amir stood motionless.

"Amir now." Louder, more commanding. "Or I kill your friend."

Amir scrambled opened the passenger door and clambered inside. Faisal followed more slowly.

"How did he find us?" the war veteran demanded.

Amir sadly held up his wrist.

"Take it off."

As Salman reached in, Faisal twitched and the gun exploded in the confines of the cab. Faisal had been shot through the left cheek, under the eye socket and slumped sideways towards Amir.

Instantaneously, the gun blasted again. Amir's head shot back and he slumped across the driver's seat; a large black mark above his left eye.

Salman reached between the bodies and picked up the watch. He propped up the intelligence officer before slamming the door. As he holstered the pistol his head was turning this way and that. The gun blasts had been really loud in the confines of the parked vehicle. His ears were still ringing with the sound. But no one came to investigate.

He clipped the watch to a bracket on the lorry next to them. Then he noticed Faisal's mobile tracker beside the van. He stamped on it and kicked it under the lorry. Then Salman ambled round to the driver's side of the van. He was waiting for a sudden challenge. He opened the door. A fine spray of blood had splattered his side of the cab. He pushed Amir's dead-weight over, to slump against the untidy shape collapsed against the passenger door. He looked round again. There was still no reaction.

The older man picked up Amir's hoody and wiped the windscreen and side window as clean as possible. One more glance round showed that nobody was coming to investigate the noise. Salman started the engine and reversed out of the parking space. He threaded the vehicle through the car park. He gained the motorway via the exit slip road. He put his foot down to make up for lost time. He was worried about speeding on a motorway. The van could do seventy quite comfortably. He kept a weather eye on the speedo. But kept one eye in his wing mirrors for any tailing cars.

Eleven minutes later the lorry left the parking slot. One minute before that Malcolm left his vehicle. He was agitated that Faisal had not reported back. He walked briskly through the HGV Park. There was no sign of 'Crescent Moon Sanitation Company' van. Also Faisal was not answering his mobile phone.

Cussing under his breath Malcolm went back to his car. He was immediately aware that the tracking device was sending out a signal. He wondered if Faisal had managed to secret himself aboard the van. The tracing monitor was still registering on the screen. The vehicle was about half a kilometre along the motorway, travelling in the same direction as before.

He radioed headquarters informing them that Faisal was missing. He also told them he was in pursuit of the target vehicle again. Within six minutes he was cruising one mile behind the tracking device, confident that because he could not see the target, they could not see him. It continued to bleep clearly on the tracking screen.

Meanwhile, well out of harm's way, Salman slowed to negotiate Junction 23 of the M5 heading south. He swung into the roundabout and made a right onto the A39 towards the next roundabout where he hung a left onto the Bristol Road. Amir's head lolled onto his shoulder. The intelligence officer's body was wedged against the dashboard. It took all Salman's strength to push the dead-weight across the seat. Now his erstwhile colleague was slumped across the back of the other cadaver.

He had made good time on the motorway, but was still cutting it fine.   To be fair, Salman was beyond much thought. He was thinking one step at a time.   Whenever he wondered if he could arm and insert the missiles by himself, he forced the idea from his mind.   Just focus on the next bit of road.

The road wriggled through Bridgewater, leaving Quantock Road, re-joining the A39 heading north.   Salman drove towards Combwich.   He by-passed the latter with a left-hand turn onto Withycombe Hill, followed by a swift right-hander onto some very narrow country lanes.   He followed Stert Drove to a staggered crossroad, bearing to the left and into an empty car park.   It was very flat and exposed to the elements.   He shunted backwards and forwards until the compass was pointing in the right direction.

Salman had no time to erect the tarpaulin.   He leapt out of the driver's seat to remove the lids from the front of the tubes.   Then clambered into the back.   He pushed the red button to elevate the roof.   He was so engrossed in getting them to the precise angle of elevation that he did not notice the car pulling up beside his vehicle.   It was only as he squeezed out of the rear seat that he became aware of human voices.

Jumping out of the vehicle, he looked round in alarm. The car was parked on the passenger side of his vehicle. He glanced at his watch: 11.54. There was no time for delay.

He ran round to the rear of the van and swung open the doors. He reached into the hammocks and rotated each warhead to activate them. At least they would all blow together. As he withdrew from inside the van, two figures stood beside him, both looking at him silently.

"Erm, they look like rockets," Ventured the man.
"Yes," replied Salman with the practised answer for such an occasion. "They are high tech sewage investigation units. Designed to run along sewers and detect broken pipes."
"Wow." He turned to his partner, "Never expected that. Hey!"
"I was wondering if you would like to help me," Salman asked innocently.
"What do you mean?" asked the man.
"Help me load the tubes."
"OK." He looked eager.
"I don't think you should," Began his partner looking along the tubes angled towards Hinkley Point. "They are pointing up."
"It makes loading easier," offered Salman.
"See," said the man enthusiastically. "I can help him."
Without waiting, Salman pushed the man beside the first tube.

"You open the hatch, once I've released the mechanism."
"OK."

They slotted the first missile in place, and began with the second meanwhile his girlfriend wandered along the van to look in at Amir once more.

The second missile was proving more stubborn than the first. The men were sweating when the girl returned.
"There is a dead man in the front of the car," she announced firmly.
"Don't be silly," patronised her partner. "He is probably sleeping."
She sighed and disappeared.
"Are you going to help me or not?" Salman really was at the point of blowing them both to kingdom come.
"Sorry. Its just she said..."
"I know. He always looks like he is dead."
Together they hauled the third rocket out of the harness and pushed it into the tube. The stranger closed the gate and Salman clamped it shut. Then he noticed that the interior light was on. He wondered if the woman had opened the passenger door. Was she examining the bodies? What could she do?
Salman looked at the rocket left in the cradle. Then at his watch: 12:01. One minute late. The young man put his hands on the last rocket. The last rocket would obliterate all forensic evidence. Without further reflection he grabbed up the remote and shouted:

"Ash-hadu an la ilaha ill-Allah.... Ash-hadu an la ilaha ill-Allah."

Then triggered the primed rockets.

All four fired immediately, incinerating Salman and the Good Samaritan. Three of them roared into the air on their way to Hinkley Point Nuclear Facility. At the same time, the last one in its sling, fired up and the van disintegrated. It totally obliterated everything within 10 metres, leaving a singed two-metre deep black crater where the van used to be.

SEVEN...

At 07:30 the fourth group pulled out of the stables. They went through the arch and onto the road. As security cameras later confirmed, Mohammed and Nadeem followed the same route as the first group through the Midlands, but continued on the M6 as far as junction 34 when they took a left onto Caton Road, the A683. They crossed the River Lune before heading north for a short while on the A589 then turned left to re-join the A683.

As they reached the Morecambe roundabout, they glimpsed the power station on the horizon. It was two large black, futuristic blocks, like something out of '2001: A Space Odyssey'. Then they turned left onto Middleton road. This twisted and turned its way through flat farmland countryside into the village of Middleton itself where they turned right following a brown campsite sign. Car Lane zig-zagged past a couple of caravan parks, if it had not been for the sat nav the boys would have been hopelessly lost. With the sea in front of them the road took a sharp left-hander and ran parallel to the sea then turned again. In the middle of that short stretch was a sandy area full of cars.

"There is nowhere to park." Nadeem rubber-necked the area. Mohammed glanced at the time.

"Eleven twenty-five. There is still plenty of time," the veteran said.

Behind them a horn blasted. Mohammed pulled over, half on the sand and half on the tarmac to allow an impatient four-by-four driver to pass.

"We cannot go far or the co-ordinates will be wrong." Mohammed tried to think.

"Can we pull off to the side of the road here?"

"It would be difficult to be private." Mohammed scanned the scene. "People will see the rockets."

"What about the caravan park?" Nadeem pointed behind them. Above the hedge caravan tops glinted in the sun. Mohammed craned round to look at the entrance.

"As long as we are near here. The calculations are precise. They are measured from the car park."

"OK. You must turn round."

Nadeem disembarked while Mohammed put it in gear. The off-side wheels spun in the sand. The van stalled. Mohammed sat back to relax. Then he turned the key and the engine fired. There was the distinct smell of burning rubber. He engaged gear. Then eased off the clutch pedal slowly. This time it gained purchase on the tarmac. The van mounted the road. He drove round the corner and pulled into the entrance of the next caravan park. Performing a tight three-point turn, he drove back towards the full car park.

Nadeem had opened the five barred gate, allowing him to drive straight into the holiday park. The 'Crescent Moon Sanitation Company' vehicle turned neatly between the first two rows of static vans then nosed in between the first two holiday homes. He was grateful that no car was parked there nor a washing line installed. Mohammed pulled in close to the boundary hedge. He opened the driver's door and stood on the ledge. He stretched himself up so he could gaze over the hedge. Looking over the vegetation, he reckoned them to be about fifty metres away from the corner of the car park, they had planned to set off the rockets.

By the time Mohammed switched off the engine, Nadeem was opening the rear door to extract the tarpaulin. Mohammed climbed down then squeezed himself onto the front bumper bar. He reached up and removed the protective caps from the front of the tubes. Then he clambered onto the rear seat to activate the elevation screws.

The front of the van began to yawn open as the well-oiled hydraulics lifted the roof away from the main frame of the vehicle.

******

Martin Hunter had lived in the holiday park since Nigel Llewellyn, his old commanding officer, loaned him the family holiday home. Martin had not been a happy bunny when made redundant from the Special Forces Unit he had served for twelve years. Initially he had turned to alcohol but at the very first regimental reunion he attended, he was set a challenge.

Nigel recruited his old sergeant major, to retrain disabled soldiers for Civvy Street. There was just one proviso; Martin would have to pass the SBS fitness test first. It was necessary for him to lead by example. It was all the motivation he needed.

The old soldier moved into the caravan and instantly began a punishing fitness regime which gradually brought his body back into shape. Even he had to admit that it was taking longer than expected. But with the offer of useful employment actually helping injured comrades-at-arms, meant that his motivation was one hundred and ten percent. This was exactly what Nigel had expected.

As Martin returned to the campsite he noticed the sanitation truck tucked in behind the first caravan as a matter of course. Then continued jogging to his van overlooking the sea. He tugged open the door and pulled himself into his Bivvy. As usual he checked the time: 11:46:32. He noted it on the graph attached to the wardrobe door. He'd made good time on the ten-mile beach yomp. Jogging on sand was far more demanding than tarmac, or indeed across rough fields.

The room had been sparsely furnished by Nigel. Martin had done nothing to improve it. There was no evidence of who might live here. It smelt strongly of unwashed male. Various items of military kit were stacked precisely on shelves. Bed sheets and blankets were neatly folded at the foot of the bed. Old habits die hard.

He took a bottle of water from the fridge and swallowed a mouthful. Something was niggling at the back of his mind. There was something unusual yet weirdly familiar about the tubes on the roof of the van he spied when he arrived home.

One thing about the modern British soldier is that they no longer wait for orders. Now they are trained to take the initiative. Adrenalin pumped into his veins for the first time in a long time. Removing the weighted backpack he went straight out of the van again. By the time he got in sight of the truck its roof was fully aligned to its target. Martin spun round and looked north. The Nuclear Power Station!

He jog trotted back to his van, picked up his phone and dialled 999.

"Hello Emergency Services which…"

"Look we may not have much time."

"Please state your name and…"

"Sergeant Major Martin Hunter of the SBS. I wish to report an imminent attack on the Heysham Nuclear Power Station. Alert Security there then…"

"Can I have your address and telephone number so…."

"Stop fucking about. There is going to be a fucking attack on the fucking power station now."

"If you use offensive language like that…"

"OK lady. I am going to leave my phone on the bed so you can trace it. I am now getting a gun. I will deal with this myself. Tell the police there is going to be a shooting at the Middleton Sands Caravan Park…Middleton Sands. Pronto. That should excite the bastards."

Martin placed the phone on the table. He pulled a tatty suitcase from the top of the wardrobe. He grabbed his bunch of keys on the hook by the door. He unlocked it. Beneath the cloths was a cloth bundle. He unwrapped the gun carefully.

The Sig Sauer P226 service pistol gleamed dully in his sun-brown hand. He went to the sink and took a box of soda crystals from the row of cleaning product. Inside was a box of 9mm ammunition wrapped in an animal skin. With practised ease he loaded the revolver and stuck it in his waistband in the small of his back. He tucked his KA-BAR Combat (Bowie) knife still in its sheath, into his belt at the front, then opened the door. The old soldier stepped into the sunlight.

******

Mohammed and Nadeem had just clipped the hatch closed on the fourth and final rocket. Mohammed looked at his watch.

"Eleven fifty-six. Four minutes to zero hour." He reached for the remote. "Will you stand behind to be a martyr or come to the front so we can continue the fight?"
"There is only one God and his name is Allah."
"May Allah the Merciful accept you into the Kingdom of Heaven with all the angels and prophets." Mohammed looked heavenward.
"I'll come with you," Nadeem suddenly decided. "Martyrdom can come in the future."

Mohammed laughed and moved the tarpaulin aside to allow him access to the front of the vehicle. Nadeem went to follow him into the narrow space. He heard something, so turned his head.

There had been a swishing sound as Martin's knife sliced the reflective material. Instantly a horrendous apparition materialised. As if by magic, a man appeared. His eyes were ablaze. His right hand extended. The gun pointing forward. Nadeem spun to follow to follow Mohammed. Martin let off three quick shots. The three slugs made a neat pattern in the centre of Nadeem's back as he tumbled between the caravan and the sanitation truck.

Mohammed turned and saw his cousin's wide-eyed expression as he toppled forward. He ran in front of the truck. The ex-soldier stomped right over the fallen victim. He raised his gun again.

Mohammed wasted vital seconds fumbling his revolver out of its holster. Martin shot three quick ones into the centre of the terrorist's chest. Then, even had time to put one in the centre of the falling man's forehead. Thus Heysham Nuclear facility was saved from attack.

SIX...

At exactly 08:00 the fifth sanitation maintenance truck left the farm. Instead of moving toward the motorway, Shami turned onto the A428 towards Bedford. Later he drove under the M11 on the northern arm of the Cambridge by-pass. They stayed on the A14 through Bury St Edmunds.

He did not see the police car parked on the bridge where the A134 joins the main carriageway. Their speed registered 42 on the hand-held speed camera. PC Dan Morgan clicked the shutter to record the evidence. He gave the thumbs up to his driver PC Mike Faraday.

The engine fired and they sped down the ramp to join the A14 half a mile behind the 'speeding' van. As they neared the offending vehicle Mike switched on the overhead blue lights and began flashing the vehicle ahead.

"Wallah," exclaimed Shami.
"What's up?" Sahid had been day dreaming.
"The police."
"Where?" Although Sahid craned his head round he could not see round the apparatus in the rear of the van. "Shall we race away?"
"No. They have a faster car. And they will call for help."

Shami put his indicator on to comply with the blue flashing lights. Through the wing mirror, he watched the police car pull over. It disappeared behind their vehicle as they stopped.

"What is happening now?" The younger man was growing uneasy.
"Take out your gun." Shami spoke very quietly. "I will shoot the one who comes to this window and you shoot the one who remains in the car."

Sahid went pale. He fumbled the gun from its holster and nearly dropped it. Breathing deeply, the younger brother carefully arranged the gun in his hand. Then, looking directly ahead; his whole frame was quivering, like a jelly. Again he tried to control his breathing.

"OK." Shami spoke quietly, calmly. "He is coming down my side of the van. Ready? Get out your side. When you hear my shot, kill the driver."

Sahid opened the passenger door in a dream. He had never shot anyone before. He rotated so his legs dangled over the kerb and slid out. He carefully clicked the door shut behind him and edged along the van, careful not to be seen from the police vehicle.

Shami rolled down his window as Dan came into view.
"You know you were speeding sir?" the Officer declared.
"Oh. Sorry officer."
"You clocked up 42 mph. This is a thirty mile an hour stretch of road. Now if you would like to step out of the van…"

The police constable stepped back to allow the driver to open the door. He saw the muzzle of a gun appear in front of the frightened face and instinctively stepped forward with his hand stretched out to say,

"That is…"

He did not finish. The first round struck him in the stomach. He stepped backwards into the road clutching his abdomen. He looked down at his hand. It had blood on it. He looked up at Shami. The second shot caught him in the shoulder. He dropped his electronic pad. Then sat down heavily staring up at his assailant with a shocked expression on his face.

Two cars screeched to a halt, trying to avoid hitting the sitting policeman. Seeing the gun the drivers changed into reverse and drove back into the other vehicle. Shami heard two shots ring out behind him. Then the police car zoomed into sight from behind the van. He swerved wide to avoid his wounded colleague and the stationery cars. He was trying to cut off their escape.

Shami fired three shots at the driver through the broken window. He saw the police office slump out of view. The police car veered off the road. It came to an abrupt halt against a garden wall. Water was gushing from the radiator.

Sahid pulled open the door and crashed into his seat.

"I shot him. But he drove the car."
"Hold tight." Shami gunned the engine. He pulled out into the road between the sprawled body and the now

stationary police car. He stamped on the accelerator. He wanted to put as much distance between themselves and the shoot-out as quickly as possible. Speeding was no longer an issue. Shooting a police officer was.

None of the other traffic gave chase. But all drivers were on their mobiles reporting the shooting or filming the event unfolding before them. Within seconds they could see their films on *YouTube*. Later some were used on the different news channels. Their moment of fame had arrived!

An unmarked police vehicle picked them up just before the A12 intersection at Ipswich and the police helicopter eight minutes later as they swung north on the final leg of their mission.

As they had shot two policemen, no restriction was placed on resources for this chase. But for the same reason all pursuing vehicles were keeping their distance. By the time they got to Yoxford there were seven cars and one helicopter in tow.

The SIS or Secret Intelligence Service, also known as MI6, were getting reports that one MI5 agent had disappeared in Worcestershire and another three were unaccounted for in Buckinghamshire. A military helicopter was sent from Birmingham District SIS Rapid-Response team. Aboard were three marksmen, ready to be deployed, just as soon as they had a location.

Shami turned off the main thoroughfare opposite Red House Farm heading towards Dunwich Forest. He went straight across the B1125 and into the forest itself. The chopper was able to keep tabs on them as they slowed and turned into the car park right in the middle of the woodland. The SIS Rapid-Response Unit was notified and they went into stealth mode to drop marksmen off at two locations east and west of the now static target.

Sahid climbed out of the passenger's side. He was still in a state of shock from the shooting. He kept playing it over and over in his head. He cringed as he realised his mistakes. He kept apologising for not killing the driver properly.

Shami was philosophical about the whole thing. He pointed out that they had got to the target area. He pointed out that they had to deliver their payload as planned. The incident about shooting two police officers would be totally insignificant in comparison. Shrugging, Shami lined the vehicle up, pointing in a SSW direction. Then he removed the tube caps from the front of the roof pipes. He then climbed into the rear of the vehicle.

As the roof lifted, the police became more alarmed. The final straw came when the two men were witnessed loading missiles into the rear of the roof tubes. Word quickly passed up the chain of command right to government. Then just as rapidly it cascaded right back down again. So by the time the two terrorists had loaded the fourth tube, three marksmen were staring unblinking down their sights.

Neither Shami nor Sahid were aware of the hit because they were shot in the head at exactly the same time. Thus the Nuclear Instillation at Sizewell had been saved from destruction, which is more than could be said for Dungeness.

FIVE...

At 08:10 the sixth van left the compound. They headed south, coincidently passing Tom's van, on the Newport Pagnell roundabout. He was ensconced in the back; connecting with the satellites. He wanted to inform Jo about Faisal's disappearance. He also needed to relay the latest from Malcolm now shadowing the suspect van. He was far too busy to notice an identical van drive right past his vehicle. Then out of sight, up the slip road onto the M1 heading south.

Immediately, they entered the 50mph speed-restricted section of the motorway. One lane was closed for road works almost as far as the London Orbital at Abbots Langley. Ikram was careful to follow the speed limit between the average speed camera system employed to enforce the temporary speed limit. His eldest brother had been booked for speeding several times and each time the car was searched and he had experienced a difficult time. So Ikram heeded Naveed's advice about the speed limit. They did not want to attract attention. Unknown to the driver, his compatriot, Shami, was to become a victim of this very problem within minutes of it going through his mind.

They made good time on the London Orbital despite the heavy traffic. They had to slow down at each major intersection, because of the volume of traffic joining this major artery. Ikram was just happy that the traffic kept moving.

Adnan closed his eyes through the entire Dartford bridge crossing. He did not gaze down on the Thames glinting far below them. He was not sure which was the worse crossing. The fear of being suspended so high above the river. Or the claustrophobic effect in the dark tunnel, knowing that the river was flowing above them. It was all so unnatural. They crossed the A2 and turned onto the M2 to Dover. Again the traffic towards the Channel port was heavy, but it kept moving and so they were more or less on schedule.

At junction 10, by Willesborough, they joined the A2070 heading south. Then turned left onto the A259 towards

Lydd Airport. They continued across this flat, featureless plain, taking the first right-hand turning into New Romney. The road zig-zagged though the little market town, before the right-hander marked Littlestone, on the B2071. Ikram drove slowly through the suburbs, past car parks and a school. Then as though they had reached the end of the Earth, with absolutely nothing ahead... they had reached the coast.

In the culture of both men, going to the seaside was not in their experience. They stopped and stared when they reached Grand Parade. There was nothing grand about it, just a shingle beach tumbling to the sea. A horn blared behind them. That broke the spell.

Ikram turned right to head south once more. The featureless shingle beach to the left and the tall, mostly modern apartment blocks to their right. These gave way to two-storey buildings which then closed in on both sides as the road changed its name to Coast Drive, somehow more inappropriate since the coast had disappeared behind some new buildings. For no logical reason the area became Greatstone-on-Sea. Then the houses on the left disappeared and the shingle beach reappeared. Then the sat nav announced their arrival at their destination on the left. There loomed an almost empty car park; tarmac on shingle.

As they slowed down Adnan read out the information board.

"The Ship Inn, Free House," he looked to the left and added. "It looks more like a toilet."
Ikram glanced left as he slowed to turn.
"That's because it is a toilet. That's just advertising for businesses near here."

The van swung into the car park then a quick right into the third parking bay on the south side. He turned the van askew in the bay so it was facing due south, then shunted backwards and forwards to align the vehicle with the Nuclear Power Station. In front of them were three huge blue litter bins.

Neither man moved in the silence that followed. They simply stared ahead. Up to that moment they had been following directions. The driver was following the voice that had been directing where to turn and when to go ahead, but now there was no voice. Now there were no orders. Ikram shook his head to break the hypnotic spell of lethargy embracing him to glance at the dashboard clock:

11.42.

"We do not have much time. Come brother, our waiting is nearly over."

He jumped out of the driver's seat and stepped round to the front of the vehicle. The wooden rail that enclosed the car park stopped in front of the van to allow access to the litter bins. For a split second Ikram wondered about pulling the van away from the bins so he did not block access from the car park. Then dismissed the thought and climbed on the front bumper to pull off the tube covers. They were quite tight so took some effort to unscrew. He collected them and took them to the recycling bins. He studied the pictures and decided that being plastic they should go in the middle bin. As they clattered into the void below an old lady shuffled towards him. She was smiling. He returned the smile. She opened her plastic bag to show a newspaper, cardboard box and green gin bottle. Ikram put them in the appropriate blue container for her.

"It's George's." She spoke slowly and clearly.

"Sorry?"

"He likes his gin, you see."

"Oh yes. See you later."

"You are such a nice young man."

"Thank you."

"Nice smile."

"Thank you. I must get on with my job... See you."

"Would you like a cup of tea?"

"Sorry?"

"I live over there." She pointed to a row of bungalows across the road. "I could make you a cup of tea."

"That's so kind of you... but we are OK. Thanks anyway."

Ikram could hear Adnan wrestling with the tarpaulin.

"I really do have to go."

He clambered into the driver's seat then squeezed himself onto the back seat. He was the biggest of all the drivers. Adaptations had been made to allow for his bulk. But he still had difficulties squeezing behind the ratchet wheels. He felt the breeze ruffle his hair as the roof began to yawn open.

Once the co-ordinate readings were met, he clambered out of the van. Adnan had finished tapping in the corner spikes, so they pulled the reflective yellow material up onto it together.

"Why did you chat to the old lady?" Adnan asked.

"It would look suspicious if I hadn't. Anyway she couldn't reach the bins and needed help."

Adnan reached up to remove the four tube catches and let the flaps fall open. Then he opened the second rear door to allow access to the missiles nesting in their webbing slings. Ikram leaned into the tight space and twisted the warheads. He heard each one click home as the detonators contacted.

They began to lift out the first one. Ikram had forgotten how awkward they were. He struggled with his end and sweat popped out on his brow. He glanced at his nephew and saw the hypnotic glaze on the younger man's face. Ikram must lead. They lifted the second one out of its hammock and began to slide it into the shaft. The sweat on Ikram's hands caused it to slip and the missile clattered to the floor.

"Wallah!" exclaimed Adnan, rudely awakened from his reverie. They both stared at the rocket gleaming below. Several seconds passed. It felt like time stood still as they waited for the blast. Nothing happened.

"Come on." Ikram was aware of the time, "Let us get this one in the launcher."

He wiped his hands on his trousers. They bent down. The rocket seemed heavier lifting it from the floor. But they were able to slide it in smoothly.

"We take a break?" Adnan queried. The older man looked at his watch.

11:54.

"No time now. Wipe the sweat off your hands."

"It was you..."

"It does not matter who it was just wipe your hands."

The veteran was annoyed with his mistake. Adnan knew he would never admit that he had done anything wrong. The older man took a rag from the tool kit and rubbed his hands before passing it to Adnan. The young man wiped his hands but was giving his uncle a strange look. The third rocket easily slid into the tube.

"Here you are." A voice cut into their private world behind the screen.

Both men froze. There, immediately behind them were an old couple. Each was holding a mug of strong tea. The 'maintenance' men looked at each other.

"We will just finish the last one," Ikram said, as they lifted the last missile out of its bed.
"See, I told you he had a nice smile."
"Yes dear."
The old couple continued to hold the tea as they slid the fourth rocket into its tube.
"Looks heavy," she observed.
"Yes dear, it does. Erm… What is it?"
"It is the latest technology for filming inside sewer pipes to find leaks."
The old man smiled. "What ever will they think of next." And shook his head in wonder.

The workmen shut and clamped the hatches on the tail end of the tubes. Then Ikram took the old lady's arm and led her back through the opening. George followed. Adnan twisted his hand backwards and forwards at his boss in a gesture of incomprehension.

"What are you doing?" Adnan hissed. "Where are you going?"

"We can have a cup of tea and watch the fireworks. Oh… bring the remote."

Adnan grabbed the launching remote and trotted after the retreating trio. They walked past the blue bins. They crossed the coast road and went into the bungalow. Once they were seated in the front room, the old couple passed them the tea they had been carrying. Adnan looked at Ikram who nodded and smiled.

The old couple hurried to the window to watch as the four rockets roared into life then soared left into the sky on their way to Dungeness Nuclear Power Station. Then before their very eyes the van disintegrated in a fierce explosion of bright yellow flames.

"Goodness me!" exclaimed George. "Whatever will they think of next?"

FOUR…

At 08:30 precisely, the last sanitation truck left the manor, heading north. As motorway cameras would later verify, they followed much the same route as some of their fellow conspirators. They joined the M1 at junction 15, the Northampton turn-off, just above Sarah's Spinney. Then continued north at a steady 70mph until they came to the

M6 intersection north of Rugby. They branched left towards Birmingham. Through the dog-leg at Hockley Heath then east until the Catshill turn onto the M5.

******

They were already being monitored on the traffic cameras. The name 'Crescent Moon Sanitation Company' had been entered by The Security Service. Tom was responsible for that. Stan, an operator at the Motorway Traffic Monitoring Unit in Birmingham, beckoned for his supervisor. John Standing crouched behind Stan and nodded. He walked back to his console and highlighted the observation to the Security Services. As far as he was concerned that was the end of the matter because another operative noticed that the eastern stretch of the M42 was devoid of traffic. That was usually the first sign of an incident. He picked up the phone to alert the traffic police of a possible accident.

******

As time went on Malcolm became more concerned about the suspect he was tailing. The signal from the sanitation van continued strong but slow. He was still unhappy about Faisal's disappearance. He decided to take a closer look at the van. He planned to pass the van, ease off the next exit slip road on Junction 11 and drift slowly down the entrance slip road to take up stations a mile behind the target once again.

296

Thus, the BMW gained on its marker. He overtook the blip on his monitor and looked round. There was no van. He realised he had been duped. They must have transferred the tracker onto another vehicle in the car park.

The security vehicle suddenly surged ahead. Hidden blue lights in the grill flashing as he sped at over 120mph to the Cheltenham interchange. It was then that he called for assistance. He asked for the backup to meet him at Costas in Strensham motorway service station. As an afterthought he asked for a female member of staff to be among the team.

He zoomed up the slip road on the hard shoulder and switched on the siren. He ignored the red lights at the top. Before screeching through the tight arc of the roundabout, weaving in and out of confused traffic. Then back down the other side. He switched off the siren but kept the lights flashing. He was heading north again. Back towards Strensham Service Station.

Unfortunately the southern access is just short of Junction 8 so he was doing 140mph towards Junction 7 for Worcester South. Again zig-zagging through the traffic. Up the slip road, negotiating the optimum curve through the traffic circle and down the other side. At such speed he had little time to dwell on any outcomes. And true to his training he maintained his breakneck speed, with one objective in mind.

With only a mile to go before he entered the slip road, Malcolm switched off the blue lights. He did not want to jeopardise Faisal's chances of survival if he were being kept captive. He now wished he had searched the area more thoroughly before following the tracker... but "Hey ho!" Malcolm thought. He was a realist.

There was little to advertise the service station. Just a plain blue 'Services' sign. The slip road veered left then directed cars right to McDonalds, Costa and the usual outlets that inhabit service stations in the UK.

Malcolm pulled into a parking lot near where he had been before. He wanted to remember all that had happened. This time, before leaving the vehicle, he secured his personal microphone and earpiece and spoke as he left the car.

"Just got here. I'll search the HGV parking area. You begin in there. Is there a female officer here?"
"Hello Malcolm," Jo greeted her officer. "Has my luck changed?"
"Jo! Great. Got you out from behind your desk eh?"
"What do you want us to do?" David wanted to know.
"Search inside for Faisal." Malcolm said. "Jo search all the ladies' loos and Davy takes the men's. OK?"
"Let's go," David said.

The trio searched the service station for the missing officer. Malcolm found the shattered remains of Faisal's Communicator. It had been smashed to smithereens in the parking bay. Probably flattened by a lorry. He reported his find to the team and began searching the bushes at the far side of the parking lot when his communicator burst into life,

"Malcolm?" Jo's voice was clear. "A 'Crescent Moon Sanitation Company' van is heading south towards us."

"What?" Malcolm asked. "It doesn't make sense... unless the driver had changed to the northbound carriageway to lose me."

"Doubt it," Jo told him. "This guy was first identified on the M42 heading east."

"Curiouser and curiouser. Probably another one."

"We think so," Jo interjected. "Just got some more bad news in... three men missing in a raid in Buckinghamshire."

"Shit. Do we know who?"

"Sorry. No details yet."

"OK. Well if there is more than one of these sanitation vans we might be under a multiple attack."

"That's our thinking," Jo confirmed. "Another report of yet another van stopped by the West Midlands Police south of Bury and they shot both police officers before doing a runner. SIS is tracking them now with their rapid response unit."

"So we can't call on the chopper..."

"Malcolm? This could be the big one."

"Faisal was right wasn't he. OK. Let's go."

"Good. Let me know as soon as you make visual."

Malcom had reached his car. He could see Jo and Davy making their way through the crowds. He drew a small circle in the air beside his head. They changed direction towards their vehicle.

"Mount up." He clambered in. "You get as near the entrance as possible in case he swings in here. I'll wait near the exit in case he just sails by."

"We're on our way. Good luck." Jo sounded jolly.

"Break a leg," David had done drama at university. "Where the hell is Faisal?"

****** ****** ******

Bashir and Bilal were totally unaware of the trap being sprung just ahead. In fact when the black BMW pulled in four cars behind them, Bashir was too busy looking at his moustache in the rear view mirror. He tipped the glass down a bit to gaze at his soul-patch. It formed a small black triangle of hair below his lower lip.

"It is better than the goatee."

"Allah will not worry if you have a big beard or a little beard when you stand before him."

"I'd never thought about that." Bashir looked shocked.

"All the religious ones have big bushy beards."

"Do you have your beard in heaven?" Bilal asked.

"I think so. Is this beard big enough to get into heaven? Should we ring Imam Imran? He will know."

"Bashir! You are so vain. It does not matter. We will be martyrs for Allah soon."

"Do you want to stand behind the van when they... you know."

"I will meet Allah proud that I have stopped this infidel country from killing any more Moslem children."

"Umm." Bashir sounded noncommittal.

"Will you stand with me?" Bilal asked knowingly.

"Oh yes. Of course." But already Bashir was planning on moving round to the side of the van before pushing the button.

They cruised passed the M50 junction to Ross-on-Wye and did not notice the black BMW slowly crawl by. They soon drifted past the next junction for Tewkesbury A438 and Evesham A46. Malcolm had left the motorway so the dark blue Ford S-MAX Titanium took up stations three cars behind. Malcolm drove slowly down the slipway and pulled in about two hundred metres behind them ready to move up should the occasion demand.

Thus the procession continued through the reshaped junctions 10, 11, 11A and the new services. Everybody settled into the monotonous rhythm of a convoy. The security cars were keeping in minimal aural contact. But they were maintaining a visual on this the last 'Crescent Moon Sanitation Company' van.

Davy had been day-dreaming a bit, then realised that he was gaining on the van.

"Think he's slowing up," Davy realised. "What's ahead?"

"Service station," Malcolm's voice echoed over his earpiece.

"That is where they like to do business," Jo reasoned.

"Stay with him," Malcolm warned. "I don't want to lose another one today."

"OK," Davy decided. "We'll follow him in."

"They may well park in HGV area, that's where I cocked up last time."

"OK. Got you." David acknowledged. "We'll follow him in.

They slowed in response to the three, two, one exit count-down signs. Then they saw the 'Welcome Break' sign telling them it was Michael Wood Service Station.

"Been here before?" David asked as he pulled up behind the van.

"Uh-uh!" voiced Jo. "Not on my usual route."

"Lorry Park is to the left. Cars to the right." Davy observed.

"Follow him. I can see you." Malcolm informed them. "I'll go into the car's parking zone. Other side of the hedge."

"He's circling round, might be leaving. No. Parking at the back. Have you got him?"

"Hedge's too dense."

"He went round to the first row as you come in," David said. "Facing north. Backing up a bit."

"I'll get back to the entrance area," Malcolm informed them. "OK. I can see the van through the hedge. I am right in line. Where are you?"

"We are about half-way down on the other side."

"I think he is lining the van up with something." Jo's observation was greeted with silence.

"What?" Finally Malcolm asked the million dollar question.

"And why?" David's question was quietly asked and silently received.

They watched as someone climbed out of the passenger side. Then he stepped up on the front of the truck. He removed the lids from the four roof containers.

"Look empty from here." Jo watched through binoculars. David gave her a sidelong glance. He could see everything clearly and wondered if the glasses were really necessary.

"The driver has disappeared over the seat," She reported. "Windows are blackened. Can't see what he is doing."

They watched Bilal wander behind the truck. Malcolm climbed out of the BMW locked it and walked nearer the hedge. He was confident that it was giving enough shelter. "Opening the back doors," he whispered.

"Roof is lifting," Jo's voice rose an octave and both men looked as the roof yawned open.

"It isn't a launcher of some kind, is it?" Malcolm voiced their worst fears.

"What the hell is their target?" asked David quietly.

"Berkeley Nuclear Power Station," Jo's voice again elicited silence. David turned to look at her. The binoculars hung round her neck, because she was studying her iPhone. Her eyes met his.

"We have to stop this," she said.

"Arm up." Malcolm commanded.

"We have a problem," David said. "We have a clear view of them but they similarly have a good view of us."

"Move." Malcolm had taken command. "I need both of you armed and ready to move sooner rather than later."

Even though Malcolm was technically of a lower rank, he was the most experienced in attack situations, so he took control. This was customary practice in MI5. He raced round to the rear of his car. He threw open the boot lid. First grabbing the blue police bullet-proof flak jacket. Flinging it across his shoulders, he struggled into it. Next he took up a 9mm police issue Walther P99 semi-automatic pistol. And checked both clips. One he slotted into the base of the hand-grip and the other he slipped into his right-hand pocket. Then he pulled on the pair of prescription goggles. Slamming shut the boot, he moved back towards the hedge, holding the pistol in both hands pointing at the ground.

"I'm armed and ready. Getting behind them through the base of the hedge." He waited for the response.

David had already pulled the car round to the second row of parked lorries. There was a space between a large delivery van and an articulated lorry. He pulled into this so they were pointing towards the target. They moved to the rear of their vehicle. Jo looked up. They could not be seen from the suspect's van.

Jo yanked open the boot. She pulled the flak jackets towards them. They struggled into their vests, checking each other when togged up. Then David broke open the arsenal. He took out his MP5SFA3 semi-automatic carbine with an EOTech 512 holographic sight attached. This he pulled up to his face to sight the scopes.

Jo picked up her GLOCK 17. She selected three clips of 9mm ammunition. The first she checked and fed into the hand-grip. The others she checked then put into her right-hand pocket. David slid the shutter down on the strongbox. It locked automatically.

That was when Malcolm's message came through.
"Nearly there," Davy replied. "I've got the MP5SFA3 and Jo's got her Glock."

"Come down each side," Malcolm instructed. "David nearest the hedge. Get as near the suspects as you can and wait for my order or until you hear gun fire."

"Good luck," Jo wished them all.

"Break a leg," David, detached as usual.

David nodded to Jo and indicated the inner hedge side. He nodded again then began to creep back towards the southern perimeter.

******

Bashir leaned into the truck and twisted each warhead in turn to make sure that they were all activated. Then he and Bilal lifted the first one out of its cradle and carefully slid it into the right-hand tube. Although the tubes were lower than the front because of the elevation, it was still an effort to lift that weight above waist height to slip it into the opening.

"They are heavier than in training," grumbled Bashir.

"Shh. One is in place..." Bilal looked at his watch. "We have eleven minutes. We can rest between each one, if you like."

Bashir gave him a hard stare. "I was just saying that they are heavy. That is all."

Bilal shut the flap and Bashir clamped it closed.

Together they pulled the second missile from its hammock and pushed it into the next tube. Bashir was sweating but did not want to say anything. Again they clamped the tube. Then they manhandled the third one out of its cradle, and into the tube.

"We rest a bit," said Bashir as he put his arm across the cradles for support.

"One more! Then you can rest."

So the final missile was pressed home. They carefully clamped the hatches in place, and then stepped back to check their handiwork. Once they were satisfied that everything was ready, Bashir quickly took up the remote control.

"I will just check the front of the van." He volunteered and took a step towards the edge of the tarpaulin.

"I am a police officer," began Malcolm as he appeared behind the terrorists, "I am armed and…"

It only took that time for Bilal to spring towards the officer. Bashir ran in the opposite direction. Malcolm shot at point-blank range into Bilal's right shoulder. It stopped his forward momentum. He fired again into his left shoulder. Bilal went down. The Security agent leapt onto the collapsing figure. He expertly rolled the groaning suspect over on to his front, pulling his arms behind him. Malcolm cuffed his hands behind his back then dragged him to his feet.

"Come on you." He spat out between gritted teeth. He stumbled as he was pushed through the gap were Bashir had vanished seconds earlier. As they emerged from between the vehicles they could see David was standing guard while Jo cuffed Bashir while he lay face down on the ground.

"Well done gang," the security chief said, "Looks like we got us some witnesses."

Berkeley Nuclear Facility was saved... on this occasion.

THREE...

When Faisal was driven off by Malcolm to try and rendezvous with the whistle-blower, Tom reported developments to Jo. She wanted all the details so she could try to persuade Ray Mingdon that MI5 should be providing sufficient backup.

It was as no surprise that twenty minutes later Tom heard from Davy Jones that he was bringing Jo as initial backup. Furthermore, The Controller had ordered that Ray Mingdon himself should oversee the operation. Thus he too was en route to join Tom at the motorway junction. The Controller had apparently authorised the availability of helicopters if they were deemed necessary.

Then came the news that Faisal had disappeared. Jo arrived soon after that. She decided not to wait for Ray Mingdon. She and Davy Jones would make tracks to support Malcolm Brainchild who was shadowing the suspect vehicle, alone, without any immediate backup.

No sooner had they gone than news of the two policemen being shot came. The significant fact for Tom was the involvement of yet another 'Crescent Moon Sanitation Company' maintenance vehicle. The helicopters promised by The Controller were scrambled to follow that van moving east. Many unusual things were happening so quickly Tom began to believe that Faisal had been right all along. This was the beginning of a big concerted attack.

Then Tom realised that the vehicle involved with the shootings had been going in a different direction. So he began to scan motorway camera systems. Soon he had tracked three separate vehicles. They all had cloned number plates. He also realised that one of the vehicles was passing exactly where Faisal had disappeared. He wondered if it were a backup for the first one. He went on to consider if Faisal had somehow sabotaged the first one. He spoke to Jo about his findings and his suspicions.

Then two unmarked police vehicles pulled up either side of his vehicle. They bounced onto the grass verge under the roundabout. Ray Mingdon stalked over to the surveillance vehicle for a briefing. It was during their chat that an urgent bleeping could be heard behind Tom. He turned to the monitor.

"Looks like Tariq's phone has been turned on."

"Co-ordinates?" Raymond asked. Tom wrote them down. As he was writing, another urgent beeping interrupted them.

"That is Khalid's phone."

"Where?"

"Same place."

"Let's go. You follow."

Then there was another urgent bleeping.

"Seven of the missing people's phones have been turned on..."

Tom shouted at the retreating back of the Section Head, who waved as he ducked into the car and was whisked off in the direction of Olney.

"...It could be a trap!" Tom yelled... to himself.

The second car had slid on the grass before skidding in fast pursuit. Swearing under his breath, Tom Canning slammed the rear door of the van. He scrambled through the cluttered van and collapsed into the driver's seat. Switching on the ignition, engaging gear and slithering off the grass verge, Tom too gave chase to the cavalry disappearing over the distant horizon.

******

As soon as the last van had driven out of the Gayhurst Manor, Naveed hurried into the main building. He rushed upstairs to the room he shared with Imran to collect his luggage. He grabbed two holdalls, at the same time scanning the room for anything he may have forgotten. Then he hurried to the waiting plain white Land Cruiser.

While Ibrahim stacked the bags in the luggage space behind the rear doors, Imran went into the main hall to arm the booby trap. There was a small sensing device tucked into the corner next to the grandfather clock, by the kitchen door. It would only go off once someone stepped in front of it.

Then he paired up all the mobile phones and batteries on the hall table. As quickly as he dared, he slid the batteries into their slots. When they were ready, he checked outside that the van was waiting for him at the foot of the steps and the gate was wide open. He knew that some of the phones would have had a homing device installed by the British Secret Service, but he had no idea which ones. Therefore, he quickly switched them all *"on"*, but some were more difficult than others. They came on one at a time. Then he ran out of the building, jumped into the vehicle screaming,

"Go. Go. Go."

The urgency of his repeated commands stirred Hussain, who crashed the gears. The Land Cruiser screeched round the tinkling fountain. It shot out of the entrance like a cork ejected from a champagne magnum. Less than thirty minutes after the seventh team had departed Gayhurst Manor was empty.

They turned right and drove directly south towards Newport Pagnell. Six minutes later two silver saloons with darkened windows flashed past going the other way.

"Ahhh! They will find my little present," Imran said in a humourless, matter-of-fact way.

"Inshallah," chorused the other occupants of the vehicle.

******

Six minutes later a silver BMW M6 Gran Coupé and a silver Ford Mondeo sped up to the clock tower of Gayhurst Manor. Raymond Mingdon emerged from the back of the BMW. He waved it through the open gates into the inner courtyard. Three armed officers leapt out of the vehicle spreading out to find cover. Ray directed the Mondeo to block the gate entrance across the outside. Four intelligence officers climbed out. Ray sent two one way and two the other, round the outside of the Manor to cover any rear entrances.

Two minutes later Tom pulled up in his Ford Transit. Ray Mingdon walked up to him.

"What kept you?" Ray could not resist the jibe.

"I didn't take the advanced driver's course like the guy driving your vehicle."

"Sour grapes! Never mind. I want you to stay out here and let me know should anything untoward happen."

"I am not happy about all this," Tom began.

"What's up?"

"There are too many of the missing phones all signalling at the same time. From in there." Tom pointed to the manor house.

"Yes. Curious."

"Or a trap."

"My guys know what they are doing. Leave this to the professionals. OK?"

"I've told you want I think. I think this is a trap."

"Enough. Josephine Pullen may like to humour your little idiosyncrasies but I admire professionalism. Now, do as you are told. Pull back a bit so you can set up your monitoring service. I'll contact you after I go in. But send me a message if there is anything, and I mean anything, I should know."

Raymond spun on his heel, dismissing Tom. He stepped round the Ford, effectively blocking the way in... or the way out...

******

Hussain maintained a constant sixty miles an hour as they joined the M1 southbound through the 50mph speed restriction zone towards the London Orbital. Once there, he followed the exit heading for Heathrow and they joined the west arm of the M25 towards London's main airport.

They had to slow as the traffic became heavier and heavier nearer the busiest airport in Europe. Although it thinned a little after that, they still made slow progress as they headed south.

Once the Heathrow directions were behind them, he started following directions for Gatwick Airport. Even though he had the sat nav, he never liked to rely on it totally. He liked to find his own way, so he only half listened, just to verify his own decisions.

******

The booby trap went off at 09:32, instantly killing one secret service officer who was entering the kitchen. This triggered a chain reaction. One after another of the garages blew up. This removed much of the evidence of the van alterations, all fingerprints and two more of the secret service agents scouring the out houses and environs.

Ray Mingdon sprinted out of the gate house arch. He vaulted the Mondeo's bonnet, just as a tongue of flame licked through the space, like the breath of a pursuing dragon.

Tom Canning was crouched over his computer screens trying to tap into any signals emanating from the suspect building when the first explosion rocked his van. He stumbled into the driver's cab to see the main building burning fiercely through the gates. As he collapsed into the driver's seat, there was an explosion in one of the barns on the right. Tom turned the key and slammed the van into reverse. The next barn shook to the percussion of another explosion. The surveillance vehicle raced backwards out of the immediate danger area.

He stopped about one hundred metres away. Then felt rather than saw the next explosion. Tearing his eyes from the column of smoke billowing above the manor house, he dialled 999. He looked up and saw someone leap over the car blocking the entrance. Then the gate house blew up. He asked for ambulances and the police.

Tom Canning reported to Thames House. Next he put in a call to Jo. Once he had finished his calls, Tom clambered out of the vehicle. He plodded up the road to see if any of his colleagues had survived the mayhem.

Three weeks later four more personnel files were placed in the "missing in action" drawer in the human resources section at Thames House.

******

At Junction 7 they followed the sweeping arm on the intersection to join the M23 to Gatwick Airport. Again the traffic was becoming heavier. They were behind schedule, but unlike the units, their timetable was a little more flexible.

They drove by the second most important London Airport on their way to the gay capital of England. After Crawley the M23 becomes the A23 but the traffic flowed more freely and they were able to make up the time lost in heavier traffic. Then they motored through the South Downs and into the congested conurbation of northern Brighton.

They drove down Grand Parade, passed St. Peter's Church and The Pavilion, majestic and strangely Oriental on the right. Ahead was the sea. It yawned in front of them like the edge of the world. They negotiated the Brighton Pier roundabout, then filtered left along Marine Parade.

The sat nav negotiated their way through the complex one-way system and into their final destination. Hussain turned north on Boundary Road, followed by a quick right onto Roedean Road and another into Marine Way. Finally steering down the cliff road to the marina itself. They did not drive towards the actual harbour, but along The Strand to the Inner Basin.

Hussain pulled into the private cul-de-sac in front of their Marine residency. Ibrahim jumped out and unpadlocked the security barrier. It dropped into its slot. The driver reversed into the private parking area. They each took a bag from the back of the vehicle and stepped through the front door Ibrahim had unlocked.

There was a luxuriously appointed lounge with a huge picture window overlooking the private berths of the Inner

Basin. Ibrahim and Naveed went back to the car to unload the rest of the luggage. Hussain went into the kitchen area and began to make tea and coffee. He also searched for snacks for his fellow travellers. They would need something before the long journey. Imran switched on the TV. He surfed until he found the Al Jazeera News programme, and there was their last home, burning on the screen, right in front of him.

"Come. Look. They found my little present."

Imran's usually frozen features were set in a broad smile. His eyes shone with pleasure. There was something really satisfying about seeing the actual result of your efforts on the little screen. He had constructed innumerable IEDs but never seen what damage they had caused. But this was different. Here in splendid Technicolor was the result of his chain bomb. He quickly realised that the entire building was destroyed. There would be no evidence left to incriminate them. The smile stayed on his lips as the others gathered round and watched in awe as what had been their home for the last fourteen months disappear in front of their eyes.

"Wallah. The infidel dies," Naveed observed.
"In Allah's name it has started," Imran added. "But we must leave soon. Quickly, get all the luggage aboard. I will booby trap the basement to take this house out as

well." And the smile stayed on his face as he disappeared downstairs.

Hussain finished his preparations in the kitchen. The other two took the bags out of the French windows that overlooked their private moorings. The Fiart Mare 50 TS was berthed, ready for the sea. Aziz and Rahman were already aboard stowing the last of the provisions bought that morning. They reached over the side to take the offered bags. Everything was almost ready.

TWO...

Lord Leyton was surprised when his driver entered the tiny study in the House of Lords private chambers before 09:00.

"Suleiman? Is there anything wrong?"

"No Your Lordship."

"Is it Her Ladyship? Is she OK?" He imagined his mother suddenly struck down.

"Yes, she is fine. I dropped you off at seven-thirty. I thought you would like some more coffee."

Kabir Anwar looked at his chauffeur with undisguised surprise.

"How did you know I had finished the thermos?"

"I know today's speech is important. I thought you might need more refreshment."

Suleiman did not say that he had only half filled the flask that morning anticipating this opportunity. Smiling at his

318

employer, he opened his small backpack and took out a coffee dispenser and two tiny Arabic cups.

"Arabic coffee! How lovely."

"And dates?"

"I love the Saudi custom of coffee and dates. So civilised."

"I agree Your Lordship. It is very civilized. But it is also traditional. The Bedouin tribes of my country would share with travellers. It is very symbolic."

His lordship laughed as he took the tiny cup and sipped it before continuing with his speech. He was making some last minute changes. He found editing so difficult. He never liked to cut anything out. But it had to be perfect to be said in this wonderful historic building. It was to be delivered at 3:00pm in Room 16 in the Palace of Westminster. It would be a key note speech on developing alternative energy sources.

He liked to work here in the early morning. Their lordships rarely turned up before the nine-thirty meetings. It had a peaceful unobtrusive atmosphere, rather like an old dusty library. He could concentrate without interruption. It still gave him a great sense of pride that he was accepted in these hallowed portals. He was humbled to be allowed to make his contribution to the adoptive country he had come to love so much.

Suleiman plied him with two more cups of coffee. Soon his lordship was deep in a dreamless slumber. The Saudi rummaged in the robes locker. He brought out the body vest. It was already loaded with Semtex packages. They just needed to be connected. His lordship had already removed his suit jacket. It was easy to slip his arms through the webbing and clip the fastenings shut at the front.

Then he drew out the wires to connect each pack of explosive to the timing device. Once the wires were pushed into the soft explosive he checked the digital timer. It was still within a second of his watch. He set the time for twelve o'clock. The dial face changed from time to count-down.

8106... 8105... 8104...

There was something hypnotic watching the figures change. Suleiman clipped the clock onto the two terminals. The suicide vest was active on the gently snoring Lord in his chambers, right at the heart of the British Parliament.

Before leaving, he threw a golden robe across the body. Anyone opening the door would assume his lordship was just taking a nap. The chauffer put the flasks and small coffee cups into his rucksack. There would be no evidence. He stepped out of the small office closing the plain wooden door behind him. With no more time to lose, Suleiman strode briskly towards the exit. He stepped out into the daylight towards the short-term car park, which was traditionally used by the less abled members.

"You can't park here you know."

"I am so sorry, but as I explained, his lordship had forgotten his speech and lunch bag. I had to take it in to him."

"I know. But you said you'd just drop it off. Not stay for half an hour."

"So sorry. But his lordship does like to talk."

"That's as may be. Look, you do this again and I'll have to clamp you."

"Thank you so much. I promise you this will never happen again. Never ever. Promise."

All the time they had been chatting, Suleiman got behind the wheel and started the engine. Now he pulled away from the disgruntled official. He looked at his watch as he turned left into the traffic on Abington Street.

09:37

Seven minutes behind schedule. But his timetable was less critical than the sanitation maintenance vans. Suleiman continued along Millbank before turning left across Lambeth Bridge then right along the Albert Embankment. He switched on the radio to see if there was any news. If there was any news at this stage, it would be only be bad. 'No news is good news'. The Saudi smiled, the English have an apt idiom for every occasion.

At Vauxhall Bridge Station he bore left then right on the A203, South Lambeth Road. The chauffer negotiated the one way system, passing near the Brixton Mosque, where some of the martyrs came from. Traffic was heavy, but kept moving. Suleiman knew he was falling further behind schedule, but was aware that time could be clawed back on the M23 as long as there were no hold-ups.

It was in the heavy congestion of Streatham High Street that he heard the breaking news item that interrupted the London radio station,

"There has been an explosion at a large Buckinghamshire country house. The emergency services are at the scene of the incident now. There has been no comment so far as to the cause of the blaze, or any news about possible casualties. We will bring you more news just as soon as we get it, so stay tuned to "*CapitalFM*"…

He felt his pulse quicken with the adrenaline rush. Events were finally happening. It had really started. Suleiman had been planning this attack on the British Mainland since the death of Osama Bin Laden. His whole life had been devoted to this one action for so long, he could not conceive a time before it.

Suleiman had engineered his job as the driver for Lord Leyton. This had given him legitimate access to the rebel mosques. No one questioned the chauffeur, because everyone was watching his lordship. He had found Gayhurst Manor near Olney. He had persuaded his lordship to buy it. It was to be an educational institution training young Moslems in practical abilities like plumbing, gas fitting, electrical skills and motor mechanics. He had recruited the people to carry out the attack and it was happening now.

"And with Allah's guiding hand England will no longer attack and kill Moslem children. This I vow on the beard of Mohammed the Prophet, may peace be upon him."

The car had driven itself through Purley and Coulsdon and it was only when it came towards to beginning of the M23 that the chauffer got it back under his conscious control again. It would be a sad twist of fate should he be responsible for any failure. Suleiman had to concentrate hard as he swept over the M25 interchange where he could begin to make up for lost time.

******

Tom Canning discovered the Bentley on its way south on the M23. The police cameras flagged it up on his monitor. The Computer Boffin had just returned from the fire at Gayhurst Manor. He contacted Mervin and Bill Fox swanning about on 'Dreamland'. He outlined what had happened at Gayhurst. It had been booby-trapped to kill British Secret Service Officers. At least that was his strong impression. That being the case he warned them about being caught in that kind of situation. Tom also pointed out that the Saudi driver was en route for the Marina as they spoke.

He asked them to report to him if anything happened at the boat. He emphasised that if they got the chance to apprehend the chauffeur then they should do this. Mervin reported that nothing was happening at the boat. Also, because of what he thought happened with Jackie he did not want to see if Abdulaziz or Abdulrahman were aboard.

Tom then contacted Emily. He told her to go directly to Thames House and report to reception. Someone would meet her and take the memory stick for further analysis. She expressed her disappointed at not meeting him but promised to return to London the following weekend.

******

Once inside the marina, Suleiman parked the Bentley in the first empty space along The Strand. He grabbed two matching holdalls from the boot. They were quite heavy. He unloaded a luggage trolley. Once balanced on the cart, it was easy to wheel the baggage along The Strand to the mews. The white van was backed up to the door. The

Saudi let himself into the empty lounge. He wheeled his luggage through to the private moorings.

Hussain jumped down to help him get his cases aboard. They heaved the trolley up the gangplank. Suleiman carried his bags one at a time below deck. Then collapsed the trolley and disappeared into his cabin.

Meanwhile, Imran Iqbal went ashore for the last time. He descended into the cellar of the marina safe house. Ten minutes late he sauntered out of the rear French windows. He stopped to place a small device behind the curtains then slid the doors shut carefully. He twisted the key and walked nonchalantly across to the luxury yacht.

Now everyone was aboard Hussain pulled the gangway clear and secured the rail. As he stowed the plank into its slot on the steering deck, Rahman cast off the two retaining ropes. Aziz switched on the twin Volvo Penta IPS 600Hp engines. He let them settle into a contented purr before easing on the throttle. The vessel pulled out of their private moorings into the Inner Basin.

They drifted below the gleaming white cliffs that epitomise the south coast of England. There was one boat ahead of them when they got to the lock. Its captain ignored them so they had to wait for him to go through first.

Ten minutes later they were chugging gently round the semi-circular east breakwater of the outer harbour. The boat ahead was travelling exceptionally slowly and they made way against her. When they reached the west breakwater, the boat ahead took an unnecessarily wide turn. Abdulaziz opened her throttles and cut round sharply in front of the other yacht. He heard the complaining horn as they made headway into the anonymity of the English Channel.

Against all the odds, they had made it...

ONE...

Despite Maryam's Romanian passport, she was in fact Palestinian. She worked for the cleaning agency contracted to clean the House of Parliament. She had been cleaning their lordship's chambers for the past three months so had developed a fairly efficient system of vacuuming into a room, once round, over the centre then out, taking the contents of rubbish bins on the way. No clearing up; no picking up papers; no folding away clothes, in fact she was nimble at vacuuming round any dropped items. Things are not what they used to be.

At 10:17 precisely, Maryam pushed her ample posterior against the door of Lord Leyton's Chamber, swinging the *Numatic NDS570 Vacuum Cleaner* round with her. It entered first, a noisy wheeled intrusion that disturbed the slumbering lord. He slumped sideways. Maria watched open-mouthed as the gown-covered apparition crash onto the floor and roll onto his back, arms akimbo.

Maryam knew exactly what his lordship was wearing. She had seen suicide vests before. Picking up the vacuum cleaner she hurried along the corridor to the nearest exit. As she trotted hastily down the stairs, Jim Sullivan blocked her way. He was her favourite security officer because he always chatted to her.

She stammered, "H-h-him have suicide bomber."
"Sorry?" Jim had a joke on the tip of his tongue. "Just a minute. What did you say?"
"Upstairs. Him have bomb." She pronounced the second "*b*".
"Are you sure?"
"I see many. My husband make them. Terrible thing."
"Your Husband? What are you talking about? Look. Show me."
"I no go there."
"Yes you will madam. If I have to drag you there myself!" And he herded her back up the steps.
"I no stay."
"OK. But show me where it is."

Reluctantly Maryam led him upstairs. She stopped at the door to the corridor and pointed down the dingy passageway. Then ducked under his raised arm and dashed downstairs. Jim watched her disappear round the first corner but decided not to give chase. Instead he walked briskly down the corridor, opening and closing each door on the way. Apologising if there was someone inside, but not staying for a chat.

When he came to Lord Leyton's Chamber he could see why Maryam had run. His lordship lay prone, arms outstretch in a cruciform shape. But what held Jim's attention was the yellow webbing encasing his upper body. It had bulging pockets. Each pocket contained an untidy brown-paper parcel. Each pouch had red and black wires linking them together. Jim lifted the walkie-talkie to his lips.

"Attention. Attention. This is Jim Sullivan. This is not a drill. Repeat. This is not a drill. Go to Red Alert immediately."

It was the first time he had called for a *Red* and his blood ran cold as he gazed down at the figure in front of him.

"Sorry, please confirm that you are asking for a Red, repeat R-E-D alert?"
"Confirm. Also call bomb disposal immediately. This is an actual emergency. Repeat, this is not a practice. This is an actual event. I will stay with the bomb until they arrive."

The handset went dead. Five seconds later the fire alarm began to ring. He could visualise all the security guards clearing the building as they had so many times in training. He could hear people on his corridor grumbling as they slowly evacuated their rooms. He knew that one or two individuals would refuse to budge because their work was more important than a fire practice.

Jim could hear his lordship's snores even though the alarms were clattering at both ends of the corridor. He moved nearer the body and saw the back-light from the dial. He leaned down and studied the numbers clicking before his eyes.

4656… 4655…4654…

He blinked to break the hypnotic effect of the count-down and lifted the handset to his mouth,
"I have an update on the bomb."
"Go ahead Jim."
"There appears to be a timer attached to the device."
"Any other information so that we can brief the bomb disposal team?"
"We have numbers on what appears to be a count-down…
4644… 4643… 4642..."
"That sounds like seconds. Erm… 60 by 60 is 3600 seconds in an hour. If that is the case the bomb is due to go off at… erm… about midday. Would you say that the bomb is due to go off at 12:00?"

"Yes. Yes. That would fit."

"Thanks Jim. In that case you can relax... a bit. We've got some time. We'll get someone up to you just as soon as we have completed the evacuation."

"Thank you."

Jim used his biro to explore the route of the wires. It all seemed very simple. There was a pair of red and black wires running from each Semtex pocket to the timing device. Another pair linking it to a battery. He knew that although it appeared simple, there could be hidden booby-traps or a subtle programme built in it that would fire the bomb if any wires or the battery were interfered with.

As he sat on the floor to ease his back, the alarms were shut off. The silence that followed was more deafening than before. Jim could hear the tick of the timer marking the countdown. He could hear his own heartbeat. Then he heard the door at the end of the corridor squeak open and several people trotting towards him. Jim scrambled to his feet.

Major Douglas Wilkins, Head of Security, came in first. Took one look at the situation and smiled at Jim.

"Well done old lad. You made the right call. OK." He spoke to the group of people who had followed him to the chambers. "Check the other chambers. Never know; one of his lordships might have slept through the din."

He stepped into the room and with a wooden probe examined the wires just as Jim had done.

"Looks simple enough. But you never know. Have you tried to move him?" Jim shook his head. "Let's see if we can get him up, shall we?"

Doug and Jim stood each side of the sleeping lord. They eased him into a sitting position. The Head of Security took a closer look at the belt.

"Seems quite loose, I wonder if…"

And he gingerly loosened the left-hand shoulder strap. Then he did the same to the right- hand one.

"You hold him steady. I'll try to ease this thing up. Doesn't seem to be attached to anything."

And very slowly he pulled the body belt upwards. Jim raised Kabir's arms so his superior could continue to pull the vest off the slumbering lord. As his hands disappeared through the armholes the unsupported peer of the realm slumped heavily onto the floor. His head hit the floor but he continued to snore.

Major Wilkins held the vest at arm's length. Jim rolled his lordship onto his side into the foetal position. He pulled the robe over him. Then he took the nearest side of the suicide vest. The two security guards cautiously carried the yellow vest between them. Doug used one hand to open the door while Jim closed them behind him.

Once on the ground floor the major barked out orders. A coat was laid across their arms to hide the contraption from any public gaze. A stretcher was dispatched to take his lordship to hospital. A security van was brought up to the side entrance. Doug and Jim climbed into the back of the people carrier.

The driver put on the blue lights and siren. They wanted to get the bomb as far away from the seat of government as possible. Twenty minutes later a bomb disposal unit deactivated the device, so the Houses of Parliament were saved from destruction for a second time in its history.

ZERO...

Three days later James Sullivan pauses outside Room U on the first floor at Westminster Palace. He knocks politely before entering. The room is empty. He has five minutes. His bug detector looks like a compact hand-held vacuum cleaner. There is a low pulsating sound as he starts behind the door. It changes pitch slightly as he reaches up to the ceiling cornices and ceiling roses. Then he bends to follow along the skirting boards. Satisfied, the security officer moves to the middle of the room. He reaches under the conference table then across the upholstered chairs. Theresa May strides confidently into the room.
"Thanks Jim. Everything alright?"
"Clean as a whistle Prime Minister."

"Excellent." She places her handbag at the head of table, "And how is everything after all the excitement."

"Fine." He pauses with his hand on the door. "All in a day's work, ma'am."

He smiles and opens the door. Mrs. May watches the door close then lifts her wrist. Only fifteen minutes. She sinks onto a cushioned chair. Her next hurdle is Prime Minister's Questions. Brexit has been bad enough. But the terrorist attack on Parliament itself is monumental; historical. This PMQ would be broadcast worldwide. The whole world watching as she justifies their actions. How much could she really admit, she wonders. But she needs to be briefed first.

Right on cue, the door opens. Lord Bolden, Parliamentary Under Secretary of State for Internal Security and Counter-Terrorism steps inside.

"Good afternoon Prime Minister. I trust you are well."

"Good afternoon Lord Bolden. I'm fine. Please sit down. Now what have you got for me?"

He settles into the chair opposite while pulling papers from his briefcase. Recognising the urgency of the situation he begins without preamble,

"All warheads have now been located. The Royal Navy's standing guard until recovery operations take place. As they were delivered on bunker-busting missiles they are buried deep, so it is proving quite difficult. However, they are retrievable. We have successfully decommissioned three, so far."

"Were they able to apprehend all the military personnel involved in selling nuclear material."

"Indeed. The general public would be absolutely horrified if they knew how much military equipment goes missing each year. A massive twenty percent of the expenditure on the military goes in the front door, then straight out of the back door."

"Can I report this to Parliament?"

"Not wise to. Fifteen arrested so far, including a brigadier and colonel. They might be persuaded to incriminate someone else during questioning. Perhaps deals can be made."

"It would be awful to admit to the world that our own military was selling to known terrorist groups."

"This is just the tip of the ice-berg. This revelation might lead for calls to appoint a body to scrutinise military stores."

"Remind me again why the bombs did not detonate."

"I have an agent in the munitions storage facility at RAF Marham in Norfolk. The night before collection she crossed the wiring inside each warhead, which made it impossible for Imran Iqbal to activate them. Although to all intents and purposes it looked as though he had. They could not explode on impact, but there was some contamination. The clean up is going to take time."

Theresa scribbled notes in the margin of her speech before asking,

"Surely they were targeting the power stations. What went wrong?"

"Three years ago we placed Ibrahim Caan into the Anwar household…"

"Have we been spying on him that long?"

"No. It wasn't him we were interested in. Suleiman Al Dossary, alias Jābir ibn-Gharsi was quickly identified when he went for work as a driver for Lord Anwar. Initially we suspected that his lordship was in cahoots with the terrorist, but it soon became apparent that he was being used. Anyway, Ibrahim ingratiated himself with Suleiman. He was recruited as cook and maintenance man at their training centre. Then, when they were making their final plans Ibrahim let it be known that he had been a geography teacher in Pakistan. They trusted him to draw up the list of co-ordinates to feed into the vehicle satnavs and targeting instruments. Obviously their launch sites had to be kosher. They had to arrive in situ as planned. However, he had two lists of targets; the actual power stations for his co-conspirators to scrutinise. But a second list with targets one mile off shore. Four bunker busting missiles landing together could have caused a lot of collateral damage. And, God forbid, in the event of one bomb actually exploding, it would minimise fatalities. These he fed into the computers on the launch vehicles on the eve of the attack."

The Prime Minister looked down at her speech. "Can't reveal any of that."

"Don't volunteer anything. Ridicule the ineffectiveness of the terrorists. Say that we believe they were unable to activate the bombs properly. Nor deliver them efficiently. It is easier to laugh at them."

She crossed out a paragraph of her speech. Then made an annotation.

"One thing bothers me though..." Mrs May began, "As you knew the targets why the hell didn't you intervene?"

"Didn't have any communications with Ibrahim. It would have been fatal for him to be carrying a phone or any other means of communications. He was embedded. That is what happens. The first I knew about it was when he phoned me from the adjacent house when Iqbal was laying his booby-traps. All I had time to do was go round and pick up the pieces."

"What is the latest as to the whereabouts of the perpetrators?"

"They are being held aboard Endeavour. A ship adapted to hold them for as long as necessary. Outside British Territorial Waters, thus outside British law."

"We're not doing anything illegal are we?"

"Not at all. America has Guantanamo Bay and we have Endeavour."

"I'm not sure..."

"Unlike the American, we do not torture our captives. Nor do we deprive them of sleep or bully them. No physical violence whatsoever."

"But..."

"We do use sodium thiopental and encourage them to talk. This is recorded to be used as leverage later. It is not permissible in court. But it is very effective for finding the truth."

"Didn't tests show that subjects could be manipulated by the questioners?"

"That's the danger. But the interrogators are aware of that danger. Also the subject can not remember what they said. It has proved very useful in the past."

"Will we have human rights people screaming for our blood?"

"If they find out… possibly. But all the time we have used these soft interrogation techniques, the more successful we have been."

"I can not mention Endeavour."

"Never. Just say that they are in a secure location and are helping the police with their enquiries."

"What about the terrorists who manned the attack vehicles."

"Five showed up at The Crescent Moon the day after the strike. They had been promised safe passage out of the country. We know the identity of the others and there is a nationwide manhunt for them. Their pictures have been circulated to all media outlets. The General Public is behind us on this and we expect strong support."

"How did they know which boat to apprehend?"

"Again Caan hid a tracking device and three smoke grenades in the engine room. When Iqbal went into the Brighton house to lay his explosives, Ibrahim followed him. We had already rented the house next door. So he entered through the large patio doors, immediately adjacent to their hideaway. To assist with the subterfuge, we had put up identical curtains. So, anyone looking from the ship would assume that he had gone into the house after Iqbal. Anyway, after the ship set sail he activated the tracker and called in bomb disposal who sanitised the Brighton house."

"You were cutting it a bit fine."

"Tell me about it. We had three police power boats lying in wait out in the channel. When the launch moved into their trap, they remotely set off the grenades. Smoke filled the vessel. It stopped dead in the water. Everyone abandoned ship. The launches appeared out of the smoke and simply picked them up. Easy in the end."

"Won't they try to exact revenge on Ibrahim Caan?"

"They can't. That's not his real name. After some time with his family I will bring him back with a new identity and embed him in another suspected terrorist cell."

"What about Faisal Khan? How is he?"

"Still in intensive care. He lost a lot of blood. If it hadn't been for Rosie Fellows he would have died. She understands our need for secrecy and has signed the Official Secrets Act."

"And Mr. Khan?"

"So far so good. I would like to offer him a role with my department. But he proved his worth in MI5. I suspect he will loyally stand by Ms Pullen."

"Won't he be badly scarred?"

"Yes. The bullet went in through his lower jaw removing a lot of bone and several teeth. It exited just in front of his ear. That shattered the hinge bone joint and removed a lot of his tongue. There is considerable trauma to his sense organs. He will undergo months of skin and tissue surgery to improve his functions as well as his youthful good looks. But those deformities would give him great credibility among members of the Al Qaeda and other terrorist groups. Any disfiguration like that, in the name of Allah, proves his loyalty. He could be really useful to us as an embedded asset in the years to come. Have to talk to him when he is fully recovered."

"What are we going to do about MI5?"

"Thank God that nincompoop Raymond Mingdon died leading that abortive attack on Gayhurst Manor. He was responsible for the deaths of three intelligence officers. A classic Cold War dinosaur. I suggest he is given a State Funeral with all the honours. But put Jo Pullen on the fast track for promotion within the department. She was tenacious in her determination to crack this case. We only just managed to stay half a step in front. She was not cowed by my threatening her career. She is the kind of person MI5 needs at the moment. I would like to suggest she be included on the Queen's honours for an MBE this year. That should give her credence with her fellow Supervisors."

"Yes." Theresa scribbled in the margins.

"But she must never know that it was I who recommended her. I might need to curtail her again in the future and if she knows I am on her side…"

"Quite." Mrs. May raised an eyebrow, "What about our very own action man?"

"Ahh! The tabloids love him. Martin Hunter should get the Victoria Cross for gallantry. The red tops have made him something of a celebrity in this otherwise depressingly horrific attack on the UK. Single-handed, the man wiped out both terrorists in that particular attack. They even nicknamed him Terror Hunter. Brilliant Boy's Own Comic stuff."

"What about you?"

"Sorry ma'am?"

"A gong?"

"No thank you ma'am. I am far more effective working in the shadows. Far more effective. No. Don't even mention me."

"OK. Anything else?"

"Not really. The official line was that these terrorists were able to make the attack. We have already foiled seven this year alone. But it illustrates the fact that we can't stop them all. Some will succeed. Perhaps you can use it to set up our own Homelands Defence Department, like the US, to co-ordinate the fight against terror."

"It's time I faced the music." Theresa May glanced at her watch again. "Thanks for the briefing."

"One last thing Prime Minister. Just like to mention that this attack was made possible because we manufacture and store nuclear material in this country. If we stopped using nuclear power..."

"Most of the Greens and Liberals support this as an environmentally friendly source of power."

"But it is potentially far more dangerous than carbon emissions. Sorry. Just bringing it to your attention. If we had no nuclear power, terrorists would have to import it themselves. This would deny them one vicious weapon to use against us."

"Finished?"

"Yes Prime Minister."

"I will mention your concerns to the Department for Business, Energy & Industrial Strategy. But don't hold your breath."

The Civil Servant began collecting his papers.

"Thank you Prime Minister."

Carefully folding her speech, the Prime Minister put it into her handbag. She stood. He stood. She raised an eyebrow. He shook his head and smiled. Theresa May walked out of Room U on her way to address the House of Commons.

After two minutes the Parliamentary Under Secretary of State left the room unnoticed.

Two weeks later, Brenda Milligan a Digital Intelligence Officer, stamped "Lost in Action" on the Personnel files for Jackie Montgomery and three other Intelligence Officers. She carried them respectfully into the archive room. On pulling out the bottom draw, she noted that it was getting quite full. Soon Records Section was going to have to extend this archive. Brenda wrote a memo and put it in the staff suggestion box. She might win the prize for the most innovative suggestion for that month. With that happy thought, she wandered back into her office to continue filing hard copies. It never ceased to amaze her how much paper work there still was in the Digital Department.

28996944R00202

Printed in Poland
by Amazon Fulfillment
Poland Sp. z o.o., Wrocław